CIPS STUDY MATTERS

ADVANCED CERTIFICATE
IN PROCUREMENT AND SUPPLY OPERATIONS

COURSE BOOK

Procurement and supply environments

i

Printed and distributed by:

The Chartered Institute of Purchasing & Supply, Easton House, Easton on the Hill, Stamford, Lincolnshire
PE9 3NZ
Tel: +44 (0) 1780 756 777
Fax: +44 (0) 1780 751 610
Email: info@cips.org
Website: www.cips.org

First edition September 2012

Contents

Preface

Welcome to your new Course Book.

Your Course Book provides detailed coverage of all topics specified in the unit content.

For a full explanation of how to use your new Course Book, turn now to page ix. And good luck in your studies!

A note on style

Throughout your Course Books you will find that we use the masculine form of personal pronouns. This convention is adopted purely for the sake of stylistic convenience – we just don't like saying 'he/she' all the time. Please don't think this reflects any kind of bias or prejudice.

September 2012

The Unit Content

The unit content is reproduced below, together with reference to the chapter in this Course Book where each topic is covered.

Unit purpose and aims

On completion of this unit, candidates will understand a range of external factors that can impact on procurement and supply operations.

This unit focuses on the wider environment that impacts on procurement and supply in a range of different types of organisations; the public, private and not for profit or third sector can all be involved in fulfilling organisational needs.

Learning outcomes, assessment criteria and indicative content

Chapter

1.0 Understand the role and scope of procurement and supply in different economic sectors

1.1 Summarise the functions of the private sector

- Definitions of organisations   1
- The size and scope of the private sector in different economies   1
- Functions of private sector organisations such as profit, growth, market share, share
  price, other financial measures, corporate and social responsibility   1

1.2 Analyse the role and scope of procurement and supply in the private sector

- Sole trade, partnerships, registered companies, incorporated and unincorporated
  companies   1
- Small and medium-sized organisations (SMEs)   1
- Multinational organisations   1
- The roles of procurement and supply in the private sector   1

1.3 Analyse the role and scope of procurement and supply in the public sector

- Defining the public sector   2
- Central and local government   2
- The functions of public sector organisations   2
- The roles of procurement and supply in the public sector   2
- Commissioning and procurement   2
- Achieving budget savings and other sources of added value   2

1.4 Explain the roles of the not for profit and third sector

- Defining the not for profit or third sector   1
- Public accountability for the not for profit and third sector   1
- The role of procurement and supply in the not for profit and third sector   1

How to Use Your Course Book

Organising your study

'Organising' is the key word: unless you are a very exceptional student, you will find a haphazard approach is insufficient, particularly if you are having to combine study with the demands of a full-time job.

A good starting point is to timetable your studies, in broad terms, between now and the date of your assessment. How many subjects are you attempting? How many chapters are there in the Course Book for each subject? Now do the sums: how many days/weeks do you have for each chapter to be studied?

Remember:

- Not every week can be regarded as a study week – you may be going on holiday, for example, or there may be weeks when the demands of your job are particularly heavy. If these can be foreseen, you should allow for them in your timetabling.
- You also need a period leading up to the assessment in which you will revise and practise what you have learned.

Once you have done the calculations, make a week-by-week timetable for yourself for each paper, allowing for study and revision of the entire unit content between now and the date of your assessment.

Getting started

Aim to find a quiet and undisturbed location for your study, and plan as far as possible to use the same period each day. Getting into a routine helps avoid wasting time. Make sure you have all the materials you need before you begin – keep interruptions to a minimum.

Using the Course Book

You should refer to the Course Book to the extent that you need it.

- If you are a newcomer to the subject, you will probably need to read through the Course Book quite thoroughly. This will be the case for most students.
- If some areas are already familiar to you – either through earlier studies or through your practical work experience – you may choose to skip sections of the Course Book.

The content of the Course Book

This Course Book has been designed to give detailed coverage of every topic in the unit content. As you will see from pages vii–viii, each topic mentioned in the unit content is dealt with in a chapter of the Course Book. For the most part the order of the Course Book follows the order of the unit content closely, though departures from this principle have occasionally been made in the interest of a logical learning order.

Each chapter begins with a reference to the assessment criteria and indicative content to be covered in the chapter. Each chapter is divided into sections, listed in the introduction to the chapter, and for the most part being actual captions from the unit content.

All of this enables you to monitor your progress through the unit content very easily and provides reassurance that you are tackling every subject that is assessable.

Each chapter contains the following features.

- Clear coverage of each topic in a concise and approachable format
- A chapter summary
- Self-test questions

The study phase

For each chapter you should begin by glancing at the main headings (listed at the start of the chapter). Then read fairly rapidly through the body of the text to absorb the main points. If it's there in the text, you can be sure it's there for a reason, so try not to skip unless the topic is one you are familiar with already.

Then return to the beginning of the chapter to start a more careful reading. You may want to take brief notes as you go along.

Test your recall and understanding of the material by attempting the self-test questions. These are accompanied by cross-references to paragraphs where you can check your answers and refresh your memory.

The revision phase

Your approach to revision should be methodical and you should aim to tackle each main area of the unit content in turn. Re-read your notes. The do some question practice. The CIPS website contains many past exam questions and you should aim to identify those that are suitable for the unit you are studying.

Additional reading

Your Course Book provides you with the key information needed for each module but CIPS strongly advocates reading as widely as possible to augment and reinforce your understanding. CIPS produces an official reading list of books, which can be downloaded from the bookshop area of the CIPS website.

To help you, we have identified one essential textbook for each subject. We recommend that you read this for additional information.

The essential textbook for this unit is *Purchasing and Supply Chain Management*, by Kenneth Lysons and Brian Farrington.

CHAPTER 1

Procurement in the Private and Third Sectors

Assessment criteria and indicative content

1.1 Summarise the functions of the private sector

- Definitions of organisations
- The size and scope of the private sector in different economies
- Functions of private sector organisations such as profit, growth, market share, share price, other financial measures, corporate and social responsibility

1.2 Analyse the role and scope of procurement and supply in the private sector

- Sole trade, partnerships, registered companies, incorporated and unincorporated companies
- Small and medium sized organisations (SMEs)
- Multinational organisations
- The roles of procurement and supply in the private sector

1.4 Explain the roles of the not for profit and third sector

- Defining the not for profit or third sector
- Public accountability for the not for profit and third sector
- The role of procurement and supply in the not for profit and third sector

Section headings

1 Defining and classifying organisations
2 Private sector organisations
3 Objectives of private sector organisations
4 The regulation of private sector procurement
5 The roles of procurement and supply
6 Third sector organisations
7 Key features of third sector procurement

Introduction

In this first chapter we examine what is meant by 'organisations' and we investigate criteria by which we can distinguish different types of organisations and economic sectors. In particular, we explain the meaning of the private sector, the public sector, and the not for profit (or third) sector.

1 Defining and classifying organisations

Defining organisations

1.1 We come across 'organisations' many times every day, and the word is very commonly used in conversation and in printed text. But what exactly do we mean by 'organisation'? How can the term be defined? What features must be present before we can say 'yes – that is an organisation'?

1.2 In some cases the absence of a clear definition might pose no problem. For example, few people would disagree with the following examples of organisations.

- A multinational company such as General Motors
- A government department such as the Department for Work and Pensions in Britain
- A charity such as Oxfam
- A university
- A professional body such as the Chartered Institute of Purchasing and Supply.

1.3 However, the need for a definition, or for a defining list of characteristics, becomes apparent in less clear-cut cases. Consider the following examples.

- A village cricket team
- A professional football club
- A school chess club
- A self-employed plumber selling his services as a 'one-man band'
- A family unit – say, a mother and father plus two young children
- A market stall run by a family – say, a mother and father plus their two teenage children

1.4 One standard text – *Organisational Behaviour* by Andrzej Huczynski and David Buchanan – offers a broad definition of organisations: '... social arrangements for the controlled performance of collective goals'.

1.5 Huczynski and Buchanan's definition suggests that the difference between organisations and other social groupings with collective goals (the family, for example) is:

- the pre-occupation with performance;
- the need for controls to ensure that performance goals are being met.

1.6 The collective goals of a business organisation might include a wide range of objectives such as: profitability, market standing or market share, productivity (efficient use of resources), innovation or social responsibility (compliance with law, ethical values and/or community expectations). Typically, senior managers will lay down strategic objectives to provide overall purpose and direction for the long term. These must then be translated into more detailed operational objectives, providing a framework within which teams and individuals can make their short-term decisions day to day.

Different ways of classifying organisations

1.7 There are various ways of classifying organisations involved in procuring goods and services.

- By *structure and ownership,* including issues of incorporation (the legal structure of the organisation), ownership, control and funding. On this basis, the economy is often divided into the private sector (eg business companies), the public sector (eg government, health authorities, police and defence forces), and the third sector: sometimes subdivided into the voluntary sector (eg churches and charities) and subscription-paid sector (eg clubs, societies and associations).

- By *primary objective.* Profit-oriented organisations (common in the private sector) aim to generate profits for their owners, or return on investment. Not-for-profit organisations (common in the public and third sectors) aim to provide public, social or charitable services, protect stakeholder interests or fulfil the purposes of their members – without aiming to make a profit from doing so. Any 'surplus' of funds is reinvested in the organisation's activity.
- By *activity:* extraction of raw materials, generation of energy, manufacturing, retail, health care, information technology, media and so on. Organisations performing different activities are likely to have different objectives, technologies and practices, in order to meet the particular challenges of their task and environment.
- By *size:* special categories are often given, for example, to small and medium enterprises (SMEs) at one end of the scale and multinational corporations (MNCs) at the other.

1.8 We will look briefly at some of these distinctions and their impact on procurement and supply chain operations in this chapter.

The private and public sectors

1.9 As most readers will be aware, a private sector organisation is one that is owned by private individuals, either few in number (such as a small family business) or very numerous (as with a large company owned by millions of private shareholders). Public sector organisations on the other hand are 'owned' by the public in general: the UK National Health Service, for example, is headed by a Government minister whose responsibility is to run the service efficiently and effectively on behalf of the State.

1.10 We will look at both sectors in detail in this chapter and the next, but some key differences between them can be summarised as follows.

1.11 In the *private sector*:

- Organisations are owned by their investors (owner/proprietors or shareholders), and controlled by directors or managers on their behalf
- Activity is funded by a combination of investment, revenue (from the sale of goods or services) and debt
- The primary purpose is the achievement of commercial objectives: generally, maximising profits for their owners, or for reinvestment in the business. Managerial decisions are assessed on the extent to which they contribute to organisational profit or shareholder wealth.
- Competition is a key factor. Several, or many, firms may offer goods or services of a particular type, with consumers free to choose between their offerings: consumer choice ensures that quality and efficiency are maintained at an acceptable level.
- The core 'constituency' served by firms is shareholders, customers and employees, all of whom are involved with the firm by choice. Firms can and must, therefore, focus their activity on meeting the needs of these few key stakeholders.

1.12 In the *public sector*:

- Organisations are owned by the government on behalf of the State, which represents the public.
- Activity is financed by the state, mainly via taxation – as well as any revenue the organisation's activities may generate.

- The primary purpose is achieving defined service levels: providing efficient and effective services to the public, often within defined budgetary constraints and sustainability strategies.
- There has traditionally been little or no competition, although some governments have sought to introduce some market disciplines (eg competitive tendering). In the absence of consumer choice, quality and efficiency are imposed by mechanisms such as regulation, customer charters, performance targets and competition for funding allocations.
- The 'constituency' of concerned stakeholders is wider and more diverse, including government, taxpayers, funding bodies, those who consume services – and society as a whole. There is a far greater need for accountability and stakeholder consultation in managing the organisation.

The size and scope of the different sectors

1.13 Looking at the big picture, economic activity can't produce *everything* that might conceivably be wanted or needed by consumers, because the resources to do so (the 'factors of production': land, natural resources, labour, capital and knowledge) are limited. Some mechanism is required to decide how these resources should be used, and what goods and services should be produced.

1.14 A **market economy** operates on the basis of supply and demand: people will purchase goods and services to satisfy their wants and needs, at a price they are able and willing to pay. Commercial organisations have to offer goods and services which are in demand, at prices which maintain that demand, in order to compete with others in the market. In other words, consumer choice decides which goods and services are produced, and at what price they can be sold. This has been the basis of the private sector, ever since commerce began with barter and trade in ancient rural economies.

1.15 However, some goods and services are perceived as essential for the wellbeing of individuals and society – such as health, education, utilities and security services – even if commercial organisations don't want to produce them, because consumers are unwilling or unable to pay the market price. In such circumstances (ie when the market mechanism of supply and demand 'fails') government must step in to control production, funded via taxation and public borrowing, so that basic goods and services are available to everyone on a free or subsidised basis. This is the basis of the public sector. In its extreme form (a *centrally planned economy)*, the government would control all factors of production: all business would be publically owned or 'nationalised'.

1.16 A **mixed economy** is one in which there is neither complete capitalist control nor complete government control of resources. Instead, the state controls essential public services and basic industries which cannot raise adequate capital investment from private sources, while at the same time supporting private enterprise and the open market in other fields.

1.17 The functions of the public sector in a mixed economy are therefore as follows.

- To provide essential goods and services which might not be provided by the private sector, owing to 'market failure'
- To redistribute wealth, via taxation, in order to provide financial support for non-wage earners such as the sick, pensioners and the unemployed
- To regulate private sector activity in the public interest
- To 'bail out' private enterprises, where necessary in the public interest. There have been several high profile examples in the recent global financial crisis: eg UK regulators being

forced to vouch for the viability of Britain's biggest home loan provider, HBOS, among fears it was facing collapse – on the same day that the US central bank had to agree to pump $US85 billion into American International Group (AIG) to prevent the failure of the world's biggest insurance company.

1.18 The balance of a mixed economy – and therefore the relative size and scope of the public or private sector – will depend partly on political factors. Communist or socialist governments (as in Cuba, China, Sweden or Norway) are more likely to support a large public sector, with government expenditure representing a higher proportion of the GDP. Capitalist societies with conservative governments are more likely to reduce the public sector (eg by privatisation of public services and industries). In highly committed 'free enterprise' economies, such as Japan and the USA, few services are provided by the state.

The third sector

1.19 As we noted earlier, the primary objective of most public sector organisations is the delivery of services, rather than the generation of profits. A number of organisations in the private sector are also operated on a not-for-profit (NFP) basis, including: charities, churches, private schools and hospitals, political parties, museums, clubs and associations, interest groups and pressure groups, trade unions and professional bodies such as CIPS. These are often identified separately as the 'third' sector of the economy (the first two being the private and public sectors).

1.20 Organisations in this sector have typically been set up to achieve a defined objective (eg for a charitable purpose or to represent the interests of a group of people) rather than to maximise profit. They usually derive their income from donations, legacies (money left to the organisation in someone's will), sponsorships and government grants and subsidies, although they may also have a trading arm to generate revenue (as in the case of 'charity shops', say). They may be owned by their members (as in a club or association) or by a trust (as in a charity), and managed by a board of trustees or directors.

1.21 We will look at the third sector separately later in this chapter.

2 Private sector organisations

2.1 To get a handle on the numerous types of organisation in the private sector, there are various classifications we can use.

- We can distinguish on the basis of ownership and control – for example, sole traders, partnerships and limited companies.
- We can distinguish on the basis of size – for example, SMEs (small and medium-sized enterprises), to large, multinational corporations such as Unilever or Microsoft.
- We can distinguish on the basis of business activity – for example, **primary industries** engaged in the extraction of raw materials, **secondary industries** engaged in manufacturing, and **tertiary industries** engaged in services.

We will look at each of these classifications, and their impact on procurement.

The constitution of private sector organisations

2.2 Private sector organisations may be formed or 'constituted' in various different ways.

- An individual may carry on a business as a sole trader.

- A group of individuals may carry on a business together by legal agreement, as a partnership.
- A potentially very large number of people may carry on a business according to specific legal requirements for 'incorporation' as a company.

We will look at each of these types of organisation in turn.

Sole tradership

2.3 A sole tradership may be an appropriate business type for a tradesperson, say, or a shopkeeper or freelance designer. There is no legal distinction between the individual person and the business entity: the individual supplies all the capital for the business, and is personally liable for its debts. (This is *not* the case for a company, as we will see later...)

2.4 The advantages and disadvantages of sole tradership are summarised in Table 1.1.

Table 1.1 *Evaluating sole tradership*

ADVANTAGES	DISADVANTAGES
Few costs or legal requirements to establish the business	The proprietor is personally liable for the business's debts
No public accountability (though financial records are required for tax purposes)	It may be difficult to get finance for the business (eg a loan by personal guarantee)
The proprietor controls all decisions for the business – and enjoys all the profits	Resources are limited to what the proprietor can personally generate

Partnership

2.5 Many sole traders find that a logical way of expanding without the formalities of incorporation is to take on one or more partners, who contribute capital and expertise to the business, and who share the managerial and financial responsibilities. A partnership is defined in UK law (Partnership Act 1890) as 'the relation which subsists between persons carrying on a business in common with a view of profit'. There must be at least two to a standard maximum of 20 partners, for a commercial partnership. (A professional practice, such as a firm of accountants or solicitors, can have any number of partners.)

2.6 Like a sole tradership (and *unlike* a company), a partnership does not have a separate legal identity from its members. This means, for example, that:

- Partners jointly own the assets of the partnership and are personally liable for its debts
- Partners are entitled to participate in management and act as agents of the firm (unlike in a company, where shareholders do not necessarily have this status)
- A change of partners terminates the old firm and begins a new one (unlike in a company, where shares can be transferred from one person to another).

2.7 The advantages and disadvantages of partnerships are summarised in Table 1.2.

Table 1.2 *Evaluating partnership*

ADVANTAGES	DISADVANTAGES
Partners contribute capital and expertise	Decision-making has to be shared or negotiated
Partners share managerial and financial responsibilities and liability	Profits have to be shared among the partners
With greater asset backing, it is often easier to raise loans than for a sole trader	Partners are generally personally liable 'without limit' for the partnership's debts
Suits professions, as members are prohibited from practising as limited companies	

Limited company

2.8 By far the most common trading vehicle in the private sector is the *limited company*. A limited company is an **incorporated** body: that is, it is considered a separate legal entity (or 'person') from its individual owners (shareholders). (The syllabus refers to the term **incorporated companies**.)

- The company can own assets, enter into contracts and incur liabilities in its own name.
- If the company incurs a debt, payment will come from the assets owned by the company. The individual owners cannot be asked to contribute to the payment from their personal funds: their liability is *limited* to the amount they have invested in the company – usually by buying shares. (Hence, a 'limited company'.)

2.9 The people who pay for shares in a company are the shareholders, also known as the members of the company. These are the company owners. As time goes by, others may be invited to subscribe for shares in the company. Any money subscribed for shares belongs to the company. The company will not normally return the money to the shareholders, other than in exceptional circumstances (eg when the company ceases to trade and is wound up).

2.10 In the UK, a company may be registered as a *public limited company ('plc')* or as a *private limited company ('Ltd')*. The key differences are as follows.

- A *public* limited company may offer its shares to the general public. (A relatively small number of public companies – known as listed companies – trade their shares on The Stock Exchange.) This is not the case for a *private* limited company, whose shareholders are generally directors of the company, or connected to it in some way. This means that PLCs are able to raise significantly larger sums of capital than private limited companies.
- A *public* limited company must have a minimum authorised share capital (the value of shares the company is allowed to issue) of £50,000, with allotted shares of at least that value, and a minimum of two members and two directors. There are no minimum capital requirements for a private limited company, and the minimum number of directors is just one.
- A *public* limited company is subject to detailed company law requirements in regard to shares, directors, annual general meetings, accounting and so on. For *private* limited companies, there is much less red tape – because the owners and managers are generally the same people.

2.11 The advantages and disadvantages of incorporation are summarised in Table 1.3.

Table 1.3 *Evaluating incorporation*

ADVANTAGES	DISADVANTAGES
Limited liability protects owners from personal liability for contracts and debts	Expense and red tape of incorporation, and the constraint of a written constitution
Shares are a stable source of finance: the amount of capital is unaffected by trading, and is not subject (like loans) to finance costs	Subject to regulation eg re public disclosure (in financial reports and accounts etc)
Directors provide the expertise the business needs, without 'diluting' ownership	Share trading can result in unwanted change of ownership

2.12 In the UK, limited companies are set up by filing a Memorandum of Association and Articles of Association with the Registrar of Companies, who (for a small fee) issues the Certificate of Incorporation. (For this reason, the syllabus uses the wording **registered companies**.) All these documents are placed on file, maintained by the Registrar, and open to inspection by the public.

- The **Memorandum of Association** defines the constitution and set up of the company. It must include the name of the company, the location of its registered office, its objects (ie the kinds of business it can engage in), a statement of limited liability, and the amount of authorised share capital.
- The **Articles of Association** define the company's internal administration, rules and procedures: how shares will be issued and managed, the rights of shareholders, requirements for shareholder meetings, the powers and remuneration of directors, payment of dividends, and division of assets if the business is wound up.

Unincorporated associations

2.13 The syllabus refers to the term unincorporated companies. We take this to mean unincorporated associations: an association of individuals formed for a particular purpose, but having no distinct legal personality. Examples include clubs and societies. Members generally have no contractual relationship with each other: they just pursue a particular interest in common under the 'umbrella' of the association. They are typically very small and their overall impact on economic activity is slight.

Small and medium enterprises (SMEs)

2.14 From your own experience, you will have gathered that private sector organisations vary widely by size: from one-person operations to small businesses to vast global conglomerates. According to a 2005 European Union definition (used for grant-aid purposes):

- A 'micro' enterprise is one which has fewer than 10 employees and an annual turnover of less than 2 million euros.
- A 'small' enterprise is one which has 10–49 employees and an annual turnover of less than 10 million euros.
- A 'medium-sized' enterprise is one which has 50–249 employees and an annual turnover of less than 50 million euros.
- A 'large-scale' enterprise employs more than 250 employees, with an annual turnover of more than 50 million euros.

2.15 Particular attention has been given to small and medium enterprises (SMEs) in recent years, because (a) they are a significant contributor to economic activity (by the above definition, some 99% of enterprises in the EU in 2005, providing around 65 million jobs), and (b) because they require financial guidance and support in order to overcome lack of economic strength in competition with larger players.

2.16 Worthington and Britton *(The Business Environment)* ascribe the resurgence in the importance of the small-firm sector to a range of factors.

- The shift from manufacturing to service industry: many services are dominated by small firms
- Increasing consumer demand for more specialised and customised (as opposed to mass produced) products, to which small firms are better able to respond
- The growth of outsourcing, where non-core activities are contracted to small specialist firms
- Reorganisation and job cutting to reduce costs, creating 'downsized' organisations
- Government policy, with initiatives designed to support SMEs in creating economic activity and jobs
- More accessible technology, allowing small firms to reach global markets (via ICT) and eroding larger firms' technological edge and economies of scale

2.17 SMEs may have an advantage over large firms in clearly defined, small markets: it would not be worth large firms entering markets where there is no scope for cost-effective mass production. Such an advantage may apply in a geographically localised market, say, or in a 'niche' market for specialist, customised or premium-quality products. In addition, the entrepreneurial nature and speed of communication in small enterprises makes them particularly well suited to innovation and invention, and they may have an advantage over larger, less flexible firms in fast-changing, high-technology markets.

2.18 On the other hand, SMEs are at a disadvantage in areas such as: raising loan and share capital (because they are a greater risk); managing cashflow (being harder hard hit by late payment or non-payments); ability to take financial risks (including investment in research and development); and dealing with bureaucratic requirements.

2.19 Large organisations are able to take advantage of economies of scale.

- Technical economies, which arise in the production process. Large undertakings can afford larger and more specialised machinery, for example, and can take advantage of the cost efficiency of mass production.
- Commercial economies, such as purchasing economies (eg through bulk purchase discounts)
- Financial economies, such as obtaining loan finance at attractive rates of interest – or being able to raise large amounts of capital via the sale of shares to the public (as a public limited company).

A firm in an industry with a large consumer market may have to grow to a certain size in order to benefit from such economies of scale, and thus to be cost-competitive with larger players.

2.20 UK government support has focused on the problems and disadvantages of SMEs, in these areas, with initiatives designed to:

- Encourage on-time payment of bills by PLCs and public sector bodies
- Relax rules and regulations applicable to SMEs
- Reduce the tax burden (eg levels of corporation tax) on small business
- Provide grants to assist SMEs in rural areas or areas of industrial decline (eg the EU SME Initiative and the Enterprise Fund)
- Provide information, advice and support (eg through the Small Business Service and Business Link network).

2.21 From the above discussion, you may be able to identify particular challenges for the procurement or supply chain function in SMEs.

- A procurement officer in an SME will work within a limited expenditure budget and tight cost controls; will need to manage cashflow closely (eg securing long credit terms from suppliers); and may have to develop a supply chain which can respond to innovation, short product lifecycles and small-quantity, fast-turnaround requirements.
- A procurement officer buying *from* an SME will need to take into account the firm's limited capacity to handle volume; its potential financial instability (if it hits problems in the midst of a supply contract); and its cashflow issues (the ethical response to which would be to pay invoices on time in full).

Multinational corporations

2.22 At the other end of the size spectrum from SMEs are multinational corporations (MNCs). An MNC is likely to be diverse both in its geographical spread and in the types of business it engages in. Organisation by divisions is common, and this presents issues of organisational structure and control. Business level strategies for component **strategic business units** (SBUs) will be a priority. Purchasing staff may well be working primarily for a particular SBU rather than for the corporation as a whole.

Sources of finance in the private sector

2.23 There are a number of key sources of finance for private sector organisations.

- Initial capital investment by the owners of the business (eg in the case of a sole trader or partnership) or by venture capitalists
- Share capital: that is, the sale of shares in the company. A public limited company (plc) will, as we have seen, be able to sell shares to the general public on the Stock Exchange. A private limited company (Ltd) can raise finance by selling shares to investment syndicates and associates (eg friends and family members).
- Retained profits resulting from the profit-generating activities of the business, such as sales: that is, profits that are 'ploughed back' into the business (rather than being withdrawn by the owners or paid out to shareholders as dividends)
- Loan finance, such as bank overdraft facilities, or bank loans and debentures (usually secured against the assets of the business)
- The sale of unneeded assets
- Government grants (eg for small business development or other projects and capital purchases).

3 Objectives of private sector organisations

Profitability

3.1 As we have already seen, the primary objective for a private sector organisation is normally to maximise profits. Profit is the difference between the selling price of a product (or the total revenue earned from selling a product) and the cost of producing the product. In other words, it is the gain or surplus left over after the manufacturer or service provider has paid all its costs.

3.2 Both buyers and suppliers seek to make a profit for a number of reasons.

- Profit means that the business has covered its costs and is not 'bleeding' money in losses.

This is important for the business to survive in the long term.

- Profit belongs to the owners or shareholders of the business, as a return on their investment: a share of profits is paid to them in the form of a 'dividend' on their shares. Strong and consistent profits are therefore important to encourage shareholders to continue to invest in the company, and to maintain the share capital of the company through a high share price (reflecting market demand for the shares).
- Profits which are not paid to shareholders ('retained profits') are available for reinvestment in the development of the business, enabling it to acquire assets, meet long-term borrowings, update plant and equipment, and build up reserves for future contingencies – without the cost and risk of borrowing funds for these purposes.

3.3 Procurement staff in a profit-seeking firm may well feel pressure to achieve the lowest possible cost when purchasing supplies – but this does not mean that they will sacrifice all other considerations in order to choose the lowest-cost option. Even in the short term this might not be the best way to achieve profits. For example, a more expensive material of higher quality might lead to lower levels of waste, rework and scrap: in the long run, it may work out cheaper than an inferior material.

3.4 More importantly, buyers must look to the longer-term benefit of their organisation, and more complex definitions of 'value'. This could mean an in-depth assessment of potential suppliers along a number of dimensions, not just price. For example, the long-term profitability of the organisation might be best served by a partnership relationship with a supplier offering technology sharing, just in time delivery, ongoing collaboration on cost reduction and process improvements – and/or other non-price advantages.

3.5 Procurement teams can, however, contribute measurably to profitability through savings on materials, inventory, and contracting and transaction costs (eg through effective negotiation and contract development, efficient management of the procurement process, and effective use of inventory management and e-procurement tools). These savings in turn contribute to bottom line profit.

3.6 If cost reductions are retained within the business, there is an immediate improvement in the bottom line. If the surplus resource is used up by budget holders, there is no direct impact on the bottom line – but there is added benefit. If an organisation is profitable it is likely to grow – and **growth** is itself a common objective of private sector organisations.

Market share

3.7 One of the key features of the private sector is the very strong influence of competition. In nearly all cases, a private sector firm will be one of several, or many, firms offering goods or services of a particular type. Securing competitive advantage, in order to win *more* customers and *better quality* customers (higher lifetime value) is therefore a key focus of private sector strategy, including supply chain management.

3.8 Competitive advantage may be defined as the ability (gained through the development, protection and leverage of distinctive competencies and resources) to deliver value to customers more efficiently or effectively than one's competitors.

3.9 Strategy guru Kenichi Ohmae *(The Mind of the Strategist)* argued that: 'What business strategy is all about is, in a word, competitive advantage. The sole purpose of strategic planning is to enable a company to gain, as efficiently as possible, a sustainable edge over its competitors.' Ohmae argued that competitive advantage is achieved by matching the strengths and resources of the corporation with the needs of the market, in such a way as to achieve superior performance, relative to competitors in the market, in areas which are perceived as critical for success in the market.

3.10 Firms may measure the success of their competitive efforts in various ways: for example, sales volume growth, sales revenue growth, or growth in the number of customers. However, the most common measure of competitive success is market penetration or market share: the percentage of the total value of sales in a market (or market segment) which is accounted for by a given product or organisation. Market share may be defined in terms of either volume (units) or value (revenue).

3.11 Market share is a key indicator of performance for many private sector organisations in competitive markets. It enables firms to identify whether increases in their sales result from the market expanding – or from their capturing customers and sales from competitors.

Shareholder value

3.12 As we noted earlier, the purpose of securing or maximising corporate profitability is not just 'profitability' for its own sake. The aim of profitability is to generate a return on the value of shareholders' investment of capital in the business, in the form of either dividends or capital growth (or both).

3.13 **Dividends** are usually paid out by companies on a regular basis, typically once or twice a year. This provides an income for the owners of the business, the shareholders.

3.14 Capital growth may accrue to the shareholders through various means.

- Retained profits being reinvested in the business
- Maintaining or enhancing the value of the company's shares in the financial markets (eg due to positive market perceptions of the company's value, management and future prospects)
- Maintaining or enhancing the value of the company's assets, such as land and buildings, plant, reputational capital, intellectual property (designs and patents), brand equity (the power of strong brands to command sales and profits) and so on – increasing the overall value or worth of the corporation.

3.15 Growth in share price is not the only financial measure that shareholders will monitor. For example, shareholders are also interested in a measure called **earnings per share**. The term 'earnings' refers to the amount of profit left over for the shareholders after all external liabilities have been satisfied (including loan interest, if any, and taxation). The earnings per share measure calculates how much of the total earnings is attributable to the holder of a single share in the company.

Corporate social responsibility (CSR)

3.16 Corporate social responsibility (CSR) is increasingly prioritised as a corporate objective in the private sector, owing to public, media and consumer pressure, and the risk of reputational damage as a result of the exposure of irresponsible corporate (and supply chain) behaviour. We will look at this concept in more detail in the later chapter on social and ethical factors.

4 The regulation of private sector procurement

The influence of government

4.1 There are four main areas in which a nation's government influences private sector organisations (quite apart from its direct influence on public sector organisations).

- Governments influence the operation of organisations: what they can and cannot produce, and how they produce it (eg in laying down restrictions on production processes in order to protect the environment).
- Governments influence the costs and revenues incurred by organisations: by the application of taxes and duties on the production and sale of certain goods, and by the effect of taxes on the general level of consumer spending.
- Governments influence organisations by the actions they take in pursuing macroeconomic objectives (eg in establishing exchange rates and interest rates, by the extent to which they stimulate aggregate demand in the economy).
- Governments influence the values and norms that are regarded as acceptable within the national culture, and hence indirectly affect the outputs produced by organisations and the ways in which organisations behave.

4.2 Governments of all persuasions accept that some regulation of the private sector generally is desirable, for the following reasons.

- Governments wish to preserve a balance between consumers and firms. Consumers must be protected in terms of service, quality and price, while firms must be prevented from charging excessive prices for essential services.
- Governments wish to promote competition, eg by preventing mergers or acquisitions which result in monopolies or the abuse of a dominant market position.
- Governments wish to assist firms to prosper, because their prosperity makes for the prosperity of the nation generally.
- Governments wish to protect national interests, eg by protecting domestic companies from unfair competition from overseas companies.

Law and regulation

4.3 There is a wide variety of law and regulation affecting the conduct of business, deriving (in the UK) from three main sources: regulations and directives issued by the European Union; statute law (Acts of Parliament); and case law (law deriving from the decisions of judges in the courts, which set principles and precedents for future decisions). In addition, there are voluntary codes of practice developed by professions and industries, and scrutiny by various regulatory bodies.

4.4 This is a particularly important area for monitoring and management by procurement organisations, because:

- The organisation's response is not 'optional' or left to managerial discretion: compliance is required and enforced by various sanctions and penalties.
- The requirements are constantly changing, as courts and tribunals define them through their decisions, and as legislators and regulatory bodies issue new provisions and amendments.

4.5 Despite attempts to increase competition and innovation in markets through a process of de-regulation (eg in financial services), there are increasing legal and political constraints on managerial decision making, in areas such as the following.

- Restricting practices that tend to stifle competition, such as the formation of agreements between corporations (eg cartels) that would prevent, restrict or distort competition; and the control of monopolies, mergers which would result in monopolies, and the abuse of a dominant market position.
- Protecting the rights of minority groups in regard to equal opportunity and diversity in employment. This is covered by a range of equal opportunity law, which typically outlaws discrimination and harassment on grounds of sex, marital status, sexual orientation, race, colour, ethnicity, religious belief, disability and age.
- Protecting the rights of employees in the workplace and employment relationship. There is a wide range of employment law, embracing issues such as workplace health and safety; working hours and leave entitlements; family-friendly flexible working arrangements; rights of consultation for worker representative or trade unions; equal treatment of part-time workers; and employee rights in the event of unfair dismissal, redundancies or transfer of undertakings.
- Protecting the rights and safety of consumers, through consumer protection law; the outlawing of unfair contract terms (eg limiting manufacturers' liability for faulty or unsafe goods); regulations on product health and safety; and so on.
- Enforcing environmental protection standards and commitments, which cover an increasing body of issues including: air and water quality, climate change and greenhouse gas emissions, agriculture, biodiversity and species protection, pesticides and hazardous chemicals, waste management, remediation of environmental impacts, impact review, and the conservation of public lands and natural resources.
- Restricting the types of products that firms can supply (eg forbidding the supply of dangerous goods) or materials and ingredients that can be used (eg forbidding the use of poisonous lead in paints used in toy manufacture).
- Restricting the uses to which firms can put personal data (eg forbidding firms from passing on customer details without their consent).
- Enforcing good corporate governance: eg via corporate, finance and tax law (and voluntary regulation).
- Preventing corruption. In the private sector, this mainly concerns the prevention of money laundering: obtaining, concealing or investing funds or property known or suspected to be the proceeds of criminal conduct or terrorist funding.

Regulation of privatised firms

4.6 Privatised firms are those that used to be in public ownership but were sold by the government into private hands. In order to ensure that public services continue to be delivered (and priced) fairly, the government has imposed a regulatory regime on these firms.

4.7 The main power wielded by regulators is concerned with limiting price rises. The regulator simply instructs the firm concerned that its price rises for a particular period must not exceed a certain percentage, which invariably is less than the general rate of inflation for that period.

4.8 Another important power arises from publicity. Naturally, the activities of a large organisation affect very large numbers of people. There is widespread interest if the regulator finds fault with any of those activities, which means that the regulator has no difficulty in gaining publicity in the media. This clearly puts pressure on the monopolist firm to fall into line and pursue 'fair' policies.

4.9 Other powers include the following.

- Issuing and renewing licences for firms wishing to operate in the market. In exceptional circumstances the regulator may withdraw a licence to operate, but this would only be in extreme cases involving (for example) a threat to public safety or persistent and large-scale failure to comply with regulatory standards.
- Setting standards of good practice
- Monitoring the activities of firms operating in the market, responding to customer complaints, and seeking to ensure that firms operate to high standards.
- Communication and promotion of market activities to maintain consumer confidence.
- Making periodic reports to the government.

5 The roles of procurement and supply

Brand values

5.1 A 'brand' is defined by marketing guru Philip Kotler as 'a name, term, sign, symbol or design, or combination of them, intended to *identify* the goods or services of one seller or group of sellers, and to *differentiate* them from those of competitors [in the perceptions of customers]'.

5.2 By developing an identifiable and distinctive brand identity, branding allows customers to develop perceptions of the brand's values (eg prestige, quality, good value, style) which support purchase decisions and – ideally – foster customer loyalty. The task of the organisation marketing a brand is to ensure that the values associated with the brand, product – or organisation as a whole – are positive, attractive, and in line with how it wants to be seen, especially in relation to its competitors.

5.3 The term 'brand values' refers to what a product or corporate brand 'stands for' in the minds of customers and other stakeholders: the core values and characteristics associated with the brand. Brand values might include value for money (such as Aldi Supermarkets), quality (such as Rolls Royce cars), design (such as Apple consumer electronics), technological innovation (such as Dyson engineering products), corporate ethics (as with The Body Shop), heritage and tradition (such as Cadbury's chocolate), entrepreneurship (such as the Virgin group) – and so on.

5.4 The term 'brand positioning' is given to the way consumers define or 'place' a brand on important attributes (like price, value, quality or trendiness), or how the brand is perceived or 'placed' relative to competing products and organisations. An organisation will often seek to determine – and influence – how its corporate image and products are perceived by customers in relation to its competitors.

5.5 Procurement strategies, policies, practices and decisions will be concerned to *support* (or not undermine) the brand values and positioning created or desired by the organisation, as part of its marketing and competitive strategy.

5.6 So, for example:

- Procurement decisions should support any quality values attached to the brand, by securing high quality inputs and contributing to quality assurance processes.
- If the brand is competitively positioned on the basis of low price or value for money, procurement will have to support this by reducing or managing the costs of inputs and supply processes, so that the organisation can keep consumer prices down and maintain some kind of profit margin.

- If the brand's core values are corporate social responsibility, ethics or environmental responsibility, procurement will have to ensure that all inputs are ethical, fairly traded and environmentally friendly, and that the supply chain is managed in an ethical and responsible way.

Alignment with suppliers

5.7 A key feature of private sector innovative procurement is the extent to which the interests of buyers and suppliers have become integrated or 'aligned'.

5.8 Simple one-to-one supply relationships (with direct suppliers) have been replaced by supply chain relationships and supply chain management: an orientation which emphasises the continuous flow of value towards the customer from first producers to end users. Rather than firms competing, the modern view is that whole supply chains compete to offer customer value (and meet customer demand) more efficiently and effectively than their competitors. Suppliers are therefore seen as essential collaborators in value delivery, competitive advantage and business success.

5.9 For this reason, traditional adversarial, transactional (one-off, commercially driven) relationships have increasingly been replaced, for important and strategic procurements, by longer-term, collaborative relationships, or supply chain partnerships.

5.10 The interests of buyers and suppliers are no longer seen as mutually exclusive, or competitive – usually based around a win-lose battle to gain the advantage over the other party on price. Instead, the interests of buyers and suppliers are viewed as potentially 'aligned': that is, broadly compatible, or aiming towards the same goals. Everyone benefits from improved supply chain performance and competitive advantage. Supply chain management is often used to pursue mutual benefits, through mechanisms such as:

- Supplier development: enhancing the capacity and capability of suppliers to meet the buyer's needs – while at the same time enhancing their business development and earning potential with other (ideally non-competing) customers
- Collaborative waste and cost reductions through the supply chain: enhancing the efficiency of all parties' operations
- Collaborative process and quality improvements through the supply chain, or continuous improvement programmes: developing all parties' performance
- Collaborative efforts to improve labour and environmental management standards through the supply chain (eg through policy development, monitoring, or seeking certification under international standards schemes): improving all parties' sustainability, reputation and reputational risk management.

5.11 In addition to 'alignment', supply chains may also seek positive 'synergy', a state in which benefits are secured by collaboration, over and above what each party could secure on its own: a possibility sometimes summed up as '2 + 2 = 5'. While each party will want to maximise its own share of value gains (its 'slice of the pie'), this end can equally well be served by working together to 'enlarge the pie'. So, for example, buyers and suppliers may bring unique resources, competencies or technology to the relationship, to enhance the success of the supply chain as a whole. Meanwhile, the *pursuit* of supply chain alignment or integration may itself be synergistic, as it increases trust, information sharing and communication, joint problem-solving and other value-adding processes.

Innovative supply chain approaches

5.12 A number of supply chain approaches developed in the private sector have come to be regarded as innovative best practice which could benefit public sector procurement.

- **Early involvement of procurement.** government departments and agencies should ensure that procurement professionals are brought in at the earliest stages of projects, where their skills and knowledge are likely to have most impact.
- **Early involvement of suppliers.** A general principle is that the objectives of a procurement should be communicated to potential suppliers at an early stage, to gauge the market's ability to deliver and explore a range of possible solutions.
- **The use of electronic procurement.** E-procurement is a significant opportunity to grasp quick savings, and underlines the successful adoption of a number of specific mechanisms in the private sector, such as e-auctions, e-marketplaces and procurement cards.
- **Pro-active contract management.** There is a need for active contract management for high value and strategically important procurement. This involves ensuring that reliable and comprehensive information is available to monitor the performance of the contractor, and taking action quickly when delivery, price and quality is at risk. It also requires a clear understanding of shared responsibilities so that when the client department has agreed to provide facilities, support or other inputs essential for the supplier to meet the terms of the contract these are provided at the right time.
- **Flexibility in the use of competition.** Formal competitive procedures are being adapted in a number of ways including: early procurement involvement; working more closely with suppliers; giving suppliers better access to information about contracts; greater use of e-procurement; explicit statement of non-price selection criteria and weightings; and improved supplier debriefing.

6 Third sector organisations

The not for profit (NFP) sector

6.1 The 'third sector' of an economy comprises non-governmental organisations (NGOs) which are operated on a not-for-profit (NFP) basis, generally reinvesting any 'surplus' from their activities to further social, environmental, cultural or other value-driven objectives. Such organisations include: charities, churches, political parties, museums, clubs and associations, co-operatives, interest, pressure and advocacy groups, trade unions and professional bodies such as CIPS.

6.2 Organisations in the NFP sector have typically been set up to achieve a defined objective (eg for a charitable or awareness-raising purpose, or to represent the interests of members) rather than to maximise profit.

6.3 NFP organisations usually derive their funding from voluntary donations, legacies (money left to the organisation in someone's will), sponsorships and government grants and subsidies. They may also have a profit-seeking trading arm to generate revenue (as in the case of 'charity shops', say).

6.4 They may be owned by their members (as in a club or association) or by a trust (as in a charity). They are typically managed by a board of trustees or directors.

The voluntary and subscription sectors

6.5   NFP organisations are sometimes subdivided into further sectors, according to their membership and funding.

- In the **voluntary sector** (eg churches, charities and interest groups), the organisations are generally controlled by a few individuals (eg trustees), but operate by voluntary contributions of funding (eg donations and grants, plus sales of product where relevant) and participation (volunteer labour). The funds are used to maintain the work.
- In the **subscription paid sector** (eg clubs, trade unions and professional bodies), the organisations are owned by the people who pay subscriptions to be members.

Objectives of third sector organisations

6.6   Obviously, the range of third sector organisations is very wide, and they may have a range of different specific purposes.

- Raising public awareness of a cause or issue (eg environmental or social pressure and interest groups)
- Political lobbying and advocacy on behalf of a cause, issue or group
- Raising funds to carry out activities (perhaps using commercial operations to generate profits, in addition to requesting grants, donations or subscriptions)
- Providing material aid and services to the public or specific beneficiaries (eg homeless or aged care charities, wildlife protection and conservation groups)
- Providing services to members (eg trade unions advocating employment rights, and professional bodies securing ethical and technical standards)
- Mobilising and involving members of the public in community projects, for mutual benefit (eg Volunteer Service Overseas).

6.7   As with public sector organisations, the range of an NFP organisation's stakeholders can therefore be wide, including: contributors (staff, volunteers, members, donors); funding bodies (sponsors, funding authorities); beneficiaries of the services or activities; the media (since activities are often 'in the public interest'); and regulatory bodies. This means that there will be multiple influences on organisational policy and decision-making.

6.8   In order to avoid loss of direction, or pressure to change direction from influential stakeholders (especially sponsors and donors), third sector organisations generally set out their objectives, policies, rules and regulations in some form of governing documents – similar to the Articles of Association of a corporation. These may take the form of a written constitution, charter, trust deed or memorandum and articles of association, setting out:

- The purpose and objectives of the organisation
- Governing principles, policies, rules and regulations for operation
- Responsibilities for management of the organisation (eg the board of trustees)
- Protocols for changing administrative provisions or ceasing operations.

6.9 Johnson, Scholes & Whittington (*Exploring Corporate Strategy*) summarise some of the key characteristics of the third sector as follows: Table 1.4.

Table 1.4 *Key characteristics of the third sector*

Objectives and expectations	• May be multiple service objectives and expectations • Expectations of funding bodies are usually very influential • May be subject to political lobbying • Multiple influences on policy: complicates strategic planning • Consultation and consensus-seeking becomes a major activity • Decision-making can be slow
Market and users	• Beneficiaries of services are not necessarily contributors of revenue or resources • Multiple stakeholders and customers • Service satisfaction is not measured readily in financial terms
Resources	• Multiple sources of funding • High proportion from sponsors and donors • Resources received in advance of service delivery, often with attached expectations • Tends towards strategic emphasis on financial or resources efficiency rather than service effectiveness • Strategies and communications may be addressed as much towards sponsors and donors as clients

6.10 You may like to browse the websites of some NGOs in areas that interest you, and see how clearly articulated their values and objectives are, and how these flow down to procurement, sourcing and corporate social responsibility policies.

7 Key features of third sector procurement

Public accountability

7.1 A significant factor affecting procurement in NFP organisations is that they are seen as performing a 'stewardship' function. That is, they are spending money that has been derived not from the organisation's own trading efforts, but from someone else's donations or taxes. In fact, funding will often come from persons or organisations not themselves benefiting from the services provided.

7.2 Procurement functions are therefore more closely scrutinised and regulated than in the private commercial sector, with a strong emphasis on accountability and stewardship.

7.3 Johnson & Scholes (*Exploring Corporate Strategy*) argue that this may cause a focus on resource efficiency at the expense of service effectiveness. In other words, there is a danger that such organisations will be less concerned to identify and satisfy the needs of their 'customers' – and more concerned with demonstrating absence of waste in their use of sponsors' funds.

7.4 Third sector organisations generally establish clear governance structures for their management – and procurement – in order to provide clarity, accountability, checks and controls on the use of funds.

Regulations impacting on charities

7.5   Third sector organisations are subject to the same general laws and regulations as other private enterprises, as discussed earlier. But they may also be subject to additional regulation, as we will illustrate in the case of charities.

7.6   The Charities Commission is the statutory regulatory body for charities in England and Wales. Its objectives (as stated on its website: www.charity-commission.gov.uk) are as follows. (If you are not based in England or Wales you should check out the regulatory regime in your own country.)

- To register charities (like the registry of companies at Companies House)
- To ensure that charities meet the legal requirements for being a charity (in order to register with the Commission), and are equipped to operate properly and within the law
- To check that charities are run for public benefit, and not for private advantage
- To ensure that charities are independent and that their trustees take their decisions free of control or undue influence from outside agencies
- To detect and remedy serious mismanagement or deliberate abuse by or within charities
- To work with charities and other regulators, to enhance public confidence in charities and the work they do (in order to ensure continuing volunteer labour and funding).

7.7   The Commission has a range of responsibilities, including:

- Gathering and maintaining information about charities on the charities register, and making information available to the general public on request
- Offering advice and guidance to charities (via a help line and site visits) on governance and compliance
- Auditing charity activities to check governance and compliance arrangements
- Investigating complaints about charities, and – in the case of mismanagement or abuse – intervening to protect the charity's assets.

What do third sector organisations buy?

7.8   With such a wide range of activities carried out by third sector organisations, the range of items procured may be correspondingly wide.

- An NFP organisation may provide services – in which case, its requirements will be the same as those for other service organisations.
- An NFP organisation may have a retail arm, in order to help it raise funds – in which case, its requirements will be the same as those for other retail organisations.
- More generally, NFP organisations will have general operating requirements: office supplies and equipment, IT support, premises management services and so on.
- More specifically, NFP organisations may have requirements for specialist supplies related to their activities. A church will need premises, furniture and supplies for its religious services, say. A charity may need collecting tins, volunteer badges, merchandise for sale and so on.

Key drivers for third sector procurement policy

7.9   Key drivers for procurement policy in third sector organisations therefore include the following.

- The values of internal and external stakeholders (including founders, staff, voluntary workers, donors and supporters), which are often directly related to the mission and purpose of the organisation.
- The need to align procurement policies and procedures with the core values, cause, issue or

theme promoted by the organisation (eg to support 'green' procurement, if the organisation is an environmental charity or lobbying group).

- The management of reputation and reputational risk. Public relations crisis, caused by some internal failure of policy or implementation, is both more likely for third sector organisations (because of the extent of scrutiny and high standards) and more significant in its impact (because of the dependence on volunteer labour, political support and discretionary funding – most of which will, in turn, be intentionally directed to the values for which the organisation purports to stand). One high-profile example of reputational damage, for example, concerned the exposure of labour exploitation practices in the supply chain for Oxfam's 'Make Poverty History' wristbands.
- The need to source inputs for a very wide range of activities, some of which pose significant logistical challenges (eg foreign aid and development work, disaster relief and so on).
- The need to act as retail or merchandise buyers, if goods are resold to raise funds. Procurement officers will therefore have to source goods of a quality, variety and distinctiveness which will appeal to consumers, at a price which allows them to make a significant 'surplus' on the sale. At the same time, there will often be ethical issues involved in dealing fairly with suppliers, and providing suppliers with a fair price for their goods (especially if, like Oxfam, for example, the organisation specifically obtains goods from developing countries and small rural suppliers, as part of their charitable activity).
- The need for differentiation (eg via best practice sustainable procurement policies, or distinctive merchandise for re-sale to raise funds) in order to compete for attention, volunteers and funding
- Limited resources. Some third-sector organisations (such as the International Red Cross) have very large procurement budgets. However, many have limited funds, and are anxious to devote as much as possible of their funding to the work for which they were formed: there is therefore a strong emphasis on cost control.
- The need for economic sustainability. The term 'non-profit' or 'not-for-profit' should not be interpreted as implying a disregard for commercial disciplines. On the contrary, such disciplines may be more important than in the private commercial sector, because of the scarcity of funds; pressure to devote as much as possible of their income to beneficiaries; or expenditure limits set by funding authorities (eg grant providers) or trustees. It is worth noting, too, that NFP organisations can enjoy a 'surplus' of income over expenditure, even if it is not described as a 'profit'. Procurement professionals therefore have a key role to play.
- The need for transparency, accountability and stewardship in the management of funds – and resulting oversight and regulation: as discussed earlier.

Chapter summary

- Organisations can be categorised by activity (industry sectors), structure and ownership (public, private), primary objective (profit and not-for-profit) or size (eg small medium enterprises).
- Private sector organisations include sole traders, partnerships and limited companies (both public and private). Many enterprises are now classed as small medium enterprises (SMEs), which face particular challenges and receive public sector support.
- Objectives of private sector organisations typically include maximisation of profits and shareholder wealth, and increase in market share. Increasingly, such organisations recognise objectives of corporate social responsibility.
- There are increasing legal and political constraints on the activities of private sector organisations.
- Private sector organisations frequently adopt a supply chain approach in which the interests of buyers and suppliers are aligned for mutual advantage.
- The third (not-for-profit) sector includes charities, churches, political parties, interest and pressure groups, clubs and associations. They may have a range of purposes and activities. The main challenges for purchasing will be limited funds and accountability in the use of those funds.

 ## Self-test questions

Numbers in brackets refer to the paragraphs where you can check your answers.

1   List key differences between private and public sector organisations. (1.11, 1.12)

2   What are the functions of the public sector in a mixed economy? (1.17)

3   In what ways may private sector firms be constituted? (2.2)

4   List advantages and disadvantages of incorporating a private sector firm. (2.11, Table 1.3)

5   What factors account for the resurgence in importance of the small-firm sector? (2.16)

6   Why is the lowest-cost option not always optimal even for a buyer pursuing profit maximisation? (3.3)

7   How do governments influence private sector organisations? (4.1)

8   How are privatised firms regulated? (4.6–4.9)

9   Distinguish between the voluntary sector and the subscription paid sector. (6.5)

10 List key characteristics of the third sector in terms of objectives and expectations. (Table 1.4)

CHAPTER 2

Procurement in the Public Sector

Assessment criteria and indicative content

1.3 Analyse the role and scope of procurement and supply in the public sector

- Defining the public sector
- Central and local government
- The functions of public sector organisations
- The roles of procurement and supply in the public sector
- Commissioning and procurement
- Achieving budget savings and other sources of added value

Section headings

1. Defining the public sector
2. The impact of economic sector on procurement
3. Responsibilities for public sector procurement
4. The regulation of public sector procurement
5. The roles of procurement and supply

Introduction

In this chapter we examine the public sector, and look at the particular requirements and considerations when undertaking procurement activities in that sector.

There is considerable variety in public procurement contexts, including different requirements for central government departments and agencies, and local government authorities. We try to give a general overview of the procurement climate and structure in each context.

We also emphasise some of the key values and objectives of public sector procurement, such as competition, accountability and value for money – which have rather different connotations in the public sector than they do in the private sector.

It is difficult to say anything substantial about public sector procurement without referring to specific institutions and regulations. In this Course Book, such examples are naturally set in a UK context. If you live outside the UK you should research the corresponding regulations in your own country.

1 Defining the public sector

Types of organisations in the public sector

1.1 There are several different types of public sector organisation.

- **Government departments** carry out the work of central government. They are financed by taxation revenue, although they may also include trading organisations (such as the Stationery Office in the UK).
- **Local government authorities** carry out the work of local service administration, financed by revenue raised predominantly from local sources.
- **Quasi-Autonomous National Government Organisations** (QUANGOs) are set up by the government as independent (non-departmental) bodies, which are nevertheless dependent on the government for their existence. UK examples include the Environment Agency, the Competition Commission and the Equality and Human Rights Commission. (In the US, QUANGO stands for Quasi-Autonomous *Non* Governmental Organisation, and you may see this version used in some text books.)
- **Public corporations** (eg the BBC) are state-owned industrial and commercial undertakings. They are run by a board accountable to the Secretary of State of a sponsoring government department, with which they agree their strategic objectives, performance targets and funding. These public enterprises are an important part of the public sector, contributing significantly to national output, employment and investment. British Coal, British Energy, the Post Office and British Steel were among them in the UK, for example, but such industries have been progressively privatised (sold into private ownership) since the 1980s.
- **Municipal enterprises** are providers of goods and services (eg leisure services, museums, parks), run by local government authorities – often in competition with the private sector. Increasingly, local councils are creating separate companies or trusts to deliver such services, allowing partnership with private investors and providers.

Financing the public sector

1.2 All sources of public sector funding derive ultimately from the taxpayer. Funds are collected in various different forms: direct taxes (taxes on income, such as the corporation tax paid by companies and the income tax paid by individuals); indirect taxes (ie taxes on expenditure, such as value added tax and excise duties); and local taxes (such as council tax and business rates).

1.3 In the UK, most of this income is collected by central government (although some of it, such as council tax, is collected by local authorities). It is the task of government, and specifically the Treasury department, to distribute the income for use in the areas prioritised by government policy.

1.4 Government agencies are provided with funds by central government for spending on their allotted responsibilities. In some cases, such agencies act as industry regulators, and when this happens, another source of their income comes from levies on the companies operating in that sector.

1.5 Where funds are collected locally, they are also spent locally, on services such as policing, rubbish collection, road maintenance and so on.

The functions of public sector organisations

1.6 The primary objectives of the public sector are *not* to make economic surplus or profits, but instead:

- To deliver essential public **services** (such as housing, healthcare, sanitation, transport, education, policing and defence) which the market might not otherwise provide equitably or fairly – to an acceptable level or quality (as expressed in government policies and customer charters)
- To encourage **national and community development**: developing education and skilling; stimulating economic activity and employment; developing technology and infrastructure (roads, communications, public spaces and so on); maintaining national security; preserving national and community heritage (both natural and human-made); supporting diversity and social inclusion (access to the benefits and opportunities offered by society); and so on
- To pursue **socio-economic goals** such as support for small and minority-owned businesses; the legislation of minimum standards for human, civil and labour rights; the promotion of work-life balance and public health; the pursuit of sustainable development, production and consumption (including sustainable procurement); environmental protection; and so on. This is often called 'corporate social responsibility' in the private sector.

1.7 In the past, the UK government has set out a procurement vision for local councils which included six key principles, reflecting these key objectives.

- Better quality services through sustainable partnerships (ie service commissioning)
- A mixed economy of service provision (ie partnering with the private and third sectors to deliver services), with ready access to a diverse and competitive range of suppliers
- Achieving continuous improvement by collaborating with partners
- Greater value from a corporate procurement strategy
- Realising community benefits
- Stimulating markets and driving innovation in the design, construction and delivery of services.

2　The impact of economic sector on procurement

2.1 Although the private sector is the focus of most procurement and supply chain literature – and arguably represents best practice in some areas of procurement and supply – the public sector is an important context for procurement operations. The spending power of public sector enterprises is enormous, and despite widespread programmes of privatisation in most developed economies, the sheer range of public sector service provision is vast: including roads, law and order, education, health and leisure services, emergency services, defence and much more.

2.2 Public and private sector organisations and environments are different in some key respects, as we noted above. The key implications for procurement have been summarised by Gary J Zenz (*Purchasing and the Management of Materials),* whose analysis forms the basis of Table 2.1, with our own points added.

2.3 The differences between public and private sector purchasing should not be overemphasised, however. Differences in objectives, organisational constraints and so on may not necessarily lead to differences in operational *procedure*.

- Public sector buyers may not be seeking to maximise profit, for example, but they will still be concerned to achieve value for money.

- Public sector buyers may not seek competitive advantage, but they will still aim to ensure the quality of inputs in order to support the quality of outputs (to fulfil the terms of a customer charter, say).
- Meanwhile, private sector buyers may not have non-economic goals as their primary objective, but they are increasingly being challenged to consider the interests of wider stakeholders in society (through pressure for corporate social responsibility).

Table 2.1 *Differences between public and private sector purchasing*

AREA OF DIFFERENCE	PRIVATE SECTOR	PUBLIC SECTOR
Objectives	Usually, to increase profit	Usually, to achieve defined service levels
Responsibility	Buyers are responsible to directors, who in turn are responsible to shareholders	Buyers are responsible ultimately to the general public
Stakeholders	Purchasing has a defined group of stakeholders to take into account.	Purchasing has to provide value to a wider range of primary and secondary stakeholders.
Activity or process	Organisational capabilities and resources used to produce goods or services	Add value through supply of outsourced or purchased products and services. (Tend not to purchase for manufacture.)
Legal restrictions	Activities are regulated by company law, employment law, product liability law etc	Most of this applies equally to public sector, but additional regulations are present too (eg EU procurement directives)
Competition	There is usually strong competition between many different firms	There is usually no competition
Value for money	Maintain lowest cost for competitive strategy, customer value and profit maximisation.	Maintain or improve service levels within value/cost parameters.
Diversity of items	Specialised stock list for defined product/service portfolio.	Wide diversity of items/resources required to provide diverse services (eg local government authority).
Publicity	Confidentiality applies in dealings between suppliers and buyers	Confidentiality is limited because of public interest in disclosure
Budgetary limits	Investment is constrained only by availability of attractive opportunities; funding can be found if prospects are good	Investment is constrained by externally imposed spending limits
Information exchange	Private sector buyers do not exchange information with other firms, because of confidentiality and competition	Public sector buyers are willing to exchange notes and use shared e-purchasing platforms, consolidate purchases etc.
Procurement policies and procedures	Tend to be organisation-specific. Private sector buyers can cut red tape when speed of action is necessary	Tend to follow legislative directives. Public sector buyers are often constrained to follow established procedures
Supplier relationships	Emphasis on long-term partnership development where possible, to support value chain.	Compulsory competitive tendering: priority to cost minimisation and efficiency, at the expense of partnership development.

2.4 An article in *Procurement Professional* journal (CIPS Australia) recently noted that: 'Key issues for the procurement profession… are as relevant for the public sector as they are for the private sector… Work is currently underway in public sectors around the world to address these issues, centred on:

- Developing standards for the assessment and ongoing development of public procurement professionals
- The greater application of strategic sourcing principles to public procurement
- The introduction of e-procurement systems.'

2.5 It should be noted that there is increasing best practice sharing between sectors, with best practice models and recommendations published by public sector bodies such as the Organisation for Government Commerce (OGC) and Sustainable Procurement Task Force, and with commitment from the public sector to learn from private sector best practice (in areas such as closer supplier relationships, supply chain innovation and procurement professionalism).

2.6 Key priorities, such as corporate social responsibility, sustainability, customer service improvement and the reduction of cost inefficiencies, operate across sectoral boundaries.

3 Responsibilities for public sector procurement

Central government procurement

3.1 In the UK, the 1999 Gershon Efficiency Review recommended centralised co-ordination of central government procurement, through the Office of Government Commerce (OGC), which was established in 2000. OGC's three main priorities were defined as: improving public services by working with departments to help them meet their efficiency targets; delivering savings in central government civil procurement; and improving the success rate of mission-critical programmes and projects. OGC therefore operates a wide-ranging programme supporting three significant activities: improving efficiency; programme and project management (PPM); and procurement.

3.2 OGC Buying Solutions is an executive agency of the OGC, providing procurement services to help public sector organisations and their private sector agents and contractors achieve value for money from procurement.

3.3 For those working in the public sector, the implications of the OGC include: greater pressure to achieve efficiency savings from procurement; greater emphasis on aggregating requirements and collaborative contracting; stronger focus on the status and role of procurement; stronger focus on professional and career development in procurement; increased involvement in contracting across the organisation; and increased involvement in cross-functional contracting teams.

Local government procurement

3.4 Unlike in central government, there is no central co-ordination of local authority procurement. Functional departments and committees are influential, and procurement's role is often limited to advising on procedures and managing clerical processes. A 2002 Audit Commission report noted that: 'It is encouraging that some authorities are using procurement as a tool for improvement, and that there is evidence of good practice. However, many authorities still need to ensure that their approach to procurement makes full use of competition and challenges current services.'

3.5 Local Government Improvement & Development (formerly known as the Improvement and Development Agency or IDeA) provides advice and guidance. It provides a range of tools and services to local authorities, including: a procurement competency framework; procurement training and development for members and officers; an e-procurement service and portal/ marketplace; best practice guidance; and a procurement toolkit.

National Health Service procurement

3.6 Until recently, the Purchasing and Supply Agency (NHS PASA) acted as a centre of expertise, knowledge and excellence in purchasing and supply matters for the health service. It advised on policy and the strategic direction of procurement, and its impact on developing healthcare, across the NHS. It also contracted on a national basis for products and services which were strategically critical to the NHS, and where sectoral aggregation of demand was thought to yield greater savings than local or regional collaboration.

3.7 The agency was closed down in April 2010, to be replaced by a more commercially-focused regime. All of its non-clinical core categories (including energy, fleet, estates and outsourcing, ICT, professional services, temporary staffing and audit) are now being handled by Buying Solutions: the national procurement partner for UK public services, and an executive agency of OGC. A series of Regional Support Units, owned by the NHS, has been set up to provide a single point of contact to suppliers in each region.

4 The regulation of public sector procurement

4.1 Spending in the public sector must comply with detailed legal regulations, and all spending decisions are subject to detailed scrutiny.

- Setting budgets for public spending begins with the Chancellor of the Exchequer, who sets overall revenue-raising and spending priorities. The budgets of public sector organisations must be set within the framework that this provides.
- Scrutiny of expenditure is carried out by the National Audit Office (which deals with central government departments and agencies) and the Audit Commission (which deals with local government authorities).

4.2 There are also a number of other regulatory bodies operating in the public sector: eg Ofsted for educational standards and the General Medical Council for health care. The purpose of these regulators is to protect public welfare and national interest, to ensure compliance with institutionalised standards – and to ensure that taxpayers' money is well spent.

4.3 Regulators may be responsible for any or all of the following issues.

- Highlighting and advising on best practice, quality standards and service levels
- Reviewing and evaluating government strategies
- Receiving reports and returns on performance, and publishing evidence-based findings
- Monitoring and auditing organisational activity for compliance to standards
- Helping customers to make informed choices and, where necessary, complaints
- Communicating and promoting the work of the sector to the public.

The impact of regulation on public procurement

4.4   The impact of regulation on public sector procurement is, broadly:

- To ensure that bought-in materials, goods and services comply with defined public standards and specifications
- To ensure that all procurement exercises are compliant with public policies, standing orders and statutory procedures – with the general aim of securing competitive supply, value for money and ethical procurement
- To ensure that all supply chain operations are compliant with law, regulation and standards in areas such as health and safety (eg in regard to manual handling or transport of dangerous goods); environmental sustainability (eg in regard to carbon emissions); employment rights (eg in regard to equal opportunity or employment protection); data protection and freedom of information.

4.5   Such regulations are common to both the public and private sectors. Public sector procurement is, however, subject to additional regulation and scrutiny.

- **EU procurement directives**, now enacted in UK law as the Public Contracts Regulations 2006 and the Public Utilities Regulations 2006
- **Anti-corruption law**, which broadly outlaws the offering and receiving of bribes and inducements which might influence, or be seen to influence, decision making by public officials (eg the Public Bodies Corrupt Practices Act 1989 and the Prevention of Corruption Act 1916)
- **Freedom of information** law (eg the Freedom of Information Act 2000), which gives the public the right to access information held by public authorities (including emails, the minutes of meetings, research and reports) – *unless* it is determined that the public interest in withholding the information is greater than the public interest in disclosing it: the 'public interest test'. Public authorities must respond promptly (within 20 days) to FOI requests, although they have 'reasonable time' to consider whether the disclosure would be in the public interest. Complaints and disputes are arbitrated by the Information Commissioner's Office
- Review by the **National Audit Office** (central government and public bodies) and the **Audit Commission** (local government authorities), whose job is to review public spending, efficiency and standards and publish reports and recommendations.

EU Public Procurement Directives

4.6   The EU Public Procurement Directives were implemented into UK law by the Public Contracts Regulations 2006, which apply to procurement by public bodies (above certain financial thresholds).

4.7   The purposes of the EU procurement directives are broadly as follows.

- To open up the choice of potential suppliers for public sector organisations and utilities, in order to stimulate competition and reduce costs
- To open up new, non-discriminatory and competitive markets for suppliers
- To ensure the free movement of goods and services within the European Union
- To ensure that public sector purchasing decisions are based on value for money (via competition) and that public sector bodies award contracts efficiently and without discrimination.

4.8   The main provisions of the regulations are as follows: Table 2.2.

Table 2.2 *Public Contracts Regulations 2006 (Public Procurement Directive)*

Advertising	• Subject to certain exceptions, public bodies must use open tendering procedures: advertising the invitation to tender according to rules designed to secure maximum publicity across the EU.
Contract award procedures	• *Open procedure*: no requirement for pre-qualification of suppliers. Tenders must be issued within six days of request by a prospective bidder. Suppliers have 52 days (minimum) to submit bids. • *Restricted procedure*: suppliers may be pre-qualified, but there must be a pre-stated range of suppliers (5–20) to whom invitations will be sent. Prospective bidders have 37 days (minimum) to register interest and submit the required information for pre-qualification. • *Negotiated procedure*: with advertisement or without (eg in the case of urgency, exclusivity agreements, or no tenders being received under other procedures). Prospective bidders have 37 days (minimum) to register their interest to negotiate. A minimum of three parties must be selected to negotiate. • *Competitive dialogue* (for large, complex contracts): a process conducted in successive stages to identify potential solutions and gradually reduce the number of tenders to be negotiated.
Award criteria	• Contracts should be let on the basis of *objective* award criteria, ensuring transparency, non-discrimination, equal treatment, and competition. • Buyers are generally obliged to award contracts on the basis of *lowest price* OR *most economically advantageous tender* (MEAT) • If MEAT is used, buyers must make this known to tender candidates and must explain the criteria that will be used to assess 'economic advantage'. • All tenderers must have reasonable, equal and timely *information* about criteria and the weighting or ranking of non-price criteria (which may include environmental and social sustainability) • The buyer may exclude bidders if they fail to meet certain defined criteria in regard to suitability, financial standing and technical competence
Right to feedback (debrief)	• The results of the tender must be notified to the Official Journal of EU • Unsuccessful bidders have the right to a de-brief within 48 days of request. The focus should be on the weaknesses that led to rejection of the bid, as well as strengths. The de-brief should *not* be used to justify the award of the contract to the successful tenderer (and, in particular, confidential information about the successful bid should *not* be disclosed).
Other provisions	Contracting authorities may use: • Framework agreements (agreeing terms governing 'standing' contracts for defined periods of up to four years) • Electronic purchasing and tendering or auction systems: completely computerised systems for quotation submission, evaluation and contract award.

4.9   The main means by which a breach of the directives may be remedied are legal action by an aggrieved supplier or contractor against a purchaser, or an action against them by a member state in the European Court of Justice. Possible 'remedies' resulting from such an action include:

- Suspension of an incomplete contract award procedure
- Setting aside of a decision in a completed contract award procedure
- An award of damages (in cases where a contract has already been entered)

4.10   It is worth being aware that this regime of compulsory open tendering has certain disadvantages. All vendors are aware that a large number of bids are likely to be made, and this may deter some suitable applicants. Moreover, since very little pre-qualification of potential vendors is allowed, some may take risks in attempting to undercut potential rivals. The result may be a contract awarded at a price that gives no incentive to high quality performance. Additionally, open tendering imposes a great administrative burden on the procurement function, which is faced with a large number of tenders to evaluate.

5 The roles of procurement and supply

Public sector supply chain drivers

5.1 In contrast to the profit focus of private sector concerns, public sector organisations have a primary orientation to achieving defined service levels: providing efficient and effective services (education, transport, healthcare) and utilities (water, power) to the public, often within defined budgetary constraints and environmental and sustainability strategies. This less intensely competitive environment allows greater information exchange, best-practice sharing and collaborative or consolidated buying and supply arrangements, such as shared e-procurement platforms and buying groups.

5.2 The range of stakeholders in public sector organisations is more diverse, including funding and user groups. This creates a more complex network of stakeholder expectations, relationships and accountabilities to be managed. A much wider diversity of items and services may also be purchased and supplied: consider a local government authority in the UK, which may be a purchaser of construction materials for use in housing or road maintenance, of dustbin lorries for refuse collection, of sporting equipment for a community leisure centre, and much more.

5.3 Public sector buyers are subject to a high level of accountability. They must ensure that appropriate processes have been followed to acquire best value for taxpayers' money; that a full 'audit trail' exists so that their actions and decisions can be vetted; and that appropriate service levels are achieved in the provision of services to members of the public. These objectives are thought to be best achieved by an insistence on competitive tendering, for contracts over a certain size (measured by contract value).

5.4 Public sector procurement (and therefore the one-to-one relationships within the supply chain) are governed by EU Directives in areas such as the compulsory use of competitive bidding, the use of e-auctions, ethical requirements (eg in regard to gifts and hospitality) and public interest disclosure of information (limiting the confidentiality of the dealings between buyers and suppliers).

5.5 As we suggested earlier, the distinction between private and public sector procurement should not be over-emphasised, since both sectors deal with inputs and broadly aspire to good practice in terms of the 'five rights'. However, you should be aware that there are some distinctive challenges in public sector purchasing.

- Public sector buyers generally have the overall objective of achieving defined service levels (rather than increasing profits, as in the private sector). 'Value' is thus defined by maintaining or improving service levels within value and cost parameters – rather than by minimising cost as part of a strategy of profit maximisation and competition.
- They are responsible ultimately to the general public, represented by the State (rather than to the shareholders of a private company, represented by its directors).
- They have to satisfy a wider range of stakeholders: managers, customers, beneficiaries of services, taxpayers, communities and so on. There will usually be a stronger emphasis

on purchasing values such as ethics, social sustainability (eg using diverse, small and local suppliers), environmental protection and so on.

- They may have a wider range of activities, and therefore a wider range of purchasing requirements. (Think of the range of items required by a school, or a local government organisation, say.)
- They are subject to established procurement procedures, and legislative directives (including the EU Public Procurement Directives, enacted in UK law as the Public Contracts Regulations). This means, for example, that competitive tendering is compulsory for placing supply contracts, unless their value is small.
- They will often be subject to budgetary constraints, cash limits and/or efficiency targets, to maximise the value obtained from public funding.

5.6   The White Paper *Setting New Standards* recognised the strategic importance of public procurement and placed an increased emphasis on securing the benefits of best purchasing practice. Specific proposals were presented for improving practice in line with the best performing private sector companies, including: an emphasis on:

- Integrated lifecycle procurement processes (or whole life contract management)
- Better management of risk
- Use of cross-functional teams
- Information sharing and collaboration
- The development of supplier relationships and a supply chain management orientation (using influence over first-tier suppliers to manage their supply chains effectively and sustainably)
- Cost reduction (especially through efficiency and collaboration with suppliers)
- The development of professional skills (eg initiatives by the Office of Government Commerce to augment the number of CIPS-qualified staff in public sector departments).
- Performance measurement (especially using balanced efficiency and effectiveness approaches such as the Procurement Excellence Model).

Commissioning and procurement

5.7   The term 'commissioning' is typically used when referring to procurement of a major public service, typically by engagement with a private sector partner. The more general term 'procurement' can be used in the same context, but can also embrace more minor purchases (such as stationery for a government department, uniforms for a local police service etc).

5.8   A key issue in the public sector is to ensure that suppliers are selected not on the grounds of political expediency, socio-economic goals, favouritism or fraud, but by transparent procedures which are open to audit and give all eligible suppliers an equal opportunity. There has been a particular emphasis on ensuring that competitive procedures are followed, as part of a process of developing the professionalism of the purchasing function.

5.9   It has also been recognised that public procurement has an important role to play in ensuring the efficient use of public funds. Policy dictates that this is to be achieved wherever possible via competition, as the best guarantee of quality and value for money.

5.10   Some form of competitive tendering is therefore used within the public sector for almost all goods purchased. For small items this usually takes the form of written quotations from selected suppliers. However, the greater the value of goods purchased, the more formal the tendering procedure. EU public procurement procedures, as we have seen, are based on formal competitive tendering to ensure openness and equality of opportunity within a competitive framework.

5.11 It is important to note that the aim of procurement is not just 'competition' for its own sake, but its judicious use to achieve *competitive supply*: the extent to which a supply arrangement provides supply which matches or exceeds requirements at a cost which represents best value in relation to a given supply market. *Competitiveness* is the strength and intensity of competition within a market, which results in genuine customer choice and potential for gains in price, quality and innovation.

5.12 One key issue is whether levels of competitiveness in a supply market result in bids which represent competitive supply, or whether there is a need to *generate* greater competition eg through: encouraging new entrants or substitute products and processes; expanding the market (eg from regional to global); collaborative buying to increase buyer power; making contracts more accessible and attractive to potential suppliers.

5.13 Compulsory competitive tendering is designed to ensure fair, non-discriminatory and competitive supplier selection, based on equality of access to tender information, selection of suppliers based on clear price (and non-price) criteria, and accountability for decisions (including feedback to unsuccessful bidders). It also supports value-for-money procurement – and procurement cost savings (as part of government efficiency targets) – by improving and maintaining the competitiveness of supply.

5.14 It has been recognised, however, that restrictive or inflexible use of competitive procedures may: discourage more innovative approaches; reinforce a risk-avoidance culture; provide an excuse for lack of expertise and professionalism; limit opportunities to achieve wider socio-economic goals through procurement; and place obstacles in the way of developing close relationships with suppliers.

5.15 The main focus has been on compliance with the EU Public Procurement Directives, emphasising the transparent use of competitive procedures, rather than necessarily the achievement of competitive supply or added value outcomes. An initial restrictive interpretation of the Directives by the OGC resulted in a negative view of the use of procurement for socio-economic purposes. EU rules do not therefore always encourage best practice procurement, in areas such as sustainability, SME and minority business participation, longer-term supply partnership relations – or indeed competitive supply.

5.16 One key challenge for public procurement is that inflexible use of competitive tendering may inhibit the development of the kinds of long-term collaborative relationships which underlie strategic procurement models. Consideration must be given to the benefits and feasibility of developing close supplier relationships within the regime.

5.17 It has long been recognised that there needs to be more constructive co-operation between customers and suppliers and that – particularly in highly specialised markets, and for complex and continuously developing requirements – longer-term partnering arrangements may be appropriate. Such partnerships will still be established by competitive tender and re-opened periodically to competition, a policy sometimes called 'partnership within competition.'

5.18 Whilst in principle 'partnership within competition' provides a viable alternative for the public sector, it risks undermining the principles of transparency, competitiveness and fraud prevention.

Such risks need to be recognised and managed, eg through greater professionalisation of the procurement function, and through the development of procedures combining dialogue with potential suppliers and formal procedures for the submission of bids. Once competitive tendering processes have been completed, close relationships may be developed between clients and suppliers on the basis of continuing competitiveness, innovation, cost and quality improvement over the duration of the contract.

5.19 Another challenge is the inflexible use of price and 'value for money' criteria in awarding competitive contracts – potentially at the expense of important criteria such as whole life costs, sustainability, or relational compatibility (eg potential for EDI links). Particular efforts may have to be made to include such criteria in specifications – which is the latest stage at which non-price criteria can be introduced.

Public accountability

5.20 The existence of multiple stakeholder objectives makes it impossible to satisfy every legitimate aspiration of the public sector's 'customers'. Managers therefore need to prioritise, and they must do so in line with policy decided upon by government. The government monitors the activities of public sector bodies to ensure that this is done.

5.21 This level of accountability impacts strongly on public procurement. One key effect is an insistence on detailed procedures and record keeping: it may be difficult later to justify a course of action which breaches defined procedures or which is poorly documented.

5.22 Specific issues in this area include: the need to record the reasons for all decisions; the need for procurement officers to declare any personal interests in procurement decisions; the need to avoid conflicts of interest; the need to secure proper authorisations; and the need generally to monitor and manage fraud risk.

5.23 However, it is often argued that the scrutiny and accountability regime also creates a 'risk avoidance' culture among public sector officials. A lack of flexibility and innovation, in seeking to minimise risks, may itself cause failure to achieve value for money. Here are some examples.

- Rigid application of procedures and use of the same terms and conditions for all contracts regardless of the nature of the requirement, market conditions and relationship with potential suppliers
- Reluctance to involve procurement at an early stage in working with clients, technical experts and users in cross-functional teams
- Reluctance to use innovative approaches such as early dialogue with suppliers over market availability and specification, visits to or presentations by potential suppliers
- Reluctance (usually by Finance) to expand the use or coverage of purchasing cards

5.24 A more flexible approach may be adopted by procurement staff, including:

- A proportional risk management approach ('control risk, not obviate it')
- Engaging external and internal auditors in dialogue about the cost and risk of over-control
- Applying directives and regulations creatively to meet customer needs
- Alerting the market to requirements early, engaging in dialogue with suppliers and improving the quality of information.

Achieving budget savings: value for money

5.25 Traditionally, measures based on value for money (VFM) have been based on prices paid and cost savings. However, a more holistic concept of VFM has been advocated. 'All public procurement of goods and services, including works, must be based on value for money... Value for money is not about achieving the lowest initial price: it is defined as *the optimum combination of whole life costs and quality*.'

5.26 This reflects an increased emphasis on:

- The importance of taking into account all aspects of cost over time, rather than lowest purchase price
- The importance of defining 'value' from the perspective of the customer, and meeting service level and quality requirements
- The importance of achieving efficiency (making best use of available resources) and effectiveness (accomplishing objectives) – in addition to economy (using the least possible resources).

5.27 Here are some ways in which procurement staff can help to achieve VFM (and not just budget savings) in public procurement.

- More efficient processing of transactions and reduced processing overheads
- Getting better VFM for goods and services purchased
- Direct negotiation with suppliers
- Collaborative or consortium buyers
- Improving project, contract and asset management
- Making procurement decisions on the basis of long-term value
- Combining competition with innovative procurement methods (while managing risks effectively)
- Utilising e-procurement and good practice
- Using tools to promote and measure VFM gains

Public private partnerships

5.28 Public private partnerships (PPP) and Private Finance Initiatives (PFI) are schemes in which private sector firms and public authorities share capital and expertise, in various structured ways, with a view to building and operating major capital and infrastructure assets. Such structured partnerships have been – and are being – used to create national infrastructure, as well as smaller projects such as hospitals, schools and barracks.

5.29 The advantages of a PPP scheme for the public sector are claimed to be as follows.

- It can lower public sector costs (owing to the way service charges paid to the private sector operator are accounted for) – and enable projects to be undertaken without having to cover capital costs from tax revenue.
- It can secure higher levels of capital expenditure and cashflow, owing to the potentially higher budget (and debt) capacity of the private sector partner. This may enable the public sector to undertake more large-scale projects than if they were prioritised under conventional public capital funding methods.
- It can tap into the creativity, expertise and existing capacity, capability and technology of private sector organisations, allowing higher levels of service to be provided to the public

(supporting the objectives of the public sector partner) – especially where service levels are secured by appropriate KPIs, or where the private sector partner is putting its own capital at risk.

- It can therefore represent excellent value for money, especially if the private partner has already invested in the required equipment, technology and so on.
- Overall, a PPP scheme can enable a public sector body to complete projects, upgrade facilities and improve public services much faster than would otherwise be possible. According to healthcare think tank the Kings Fund, for example, the physical condition of most hospitals is now 'vastly improved' thanks to such partnerships.

5.30 On the other hand:

- Critics of PPP argue that the public sector may be surrendering control of the project, with the risk of lower levels of service, public accountability and consideration of environmental and social sustainability objectives.
- PFI contracts can represent poor value for money and may saddle the public sector with unsustainable financial commitments for decades to come: some hospital authorities have found it too expensive to pay the annual charges to private sector contractors for building and servicing new hospitals, for example.
- The scheme may be unsustainably inflexible, because it ties public services into 20–30 year contracts – despite the fact that it is difficult to plan for changes in demand and service provision over such a long planning horizon.
- Trade unions have claimed that some PPP structures lead to poorer services, because private companies maintain facilities as cheaply as possible in order to maximise their profits.
- The pay and conditions of cleaners, catering and security staff in facilities operated by the private sector are typically worse than their counterparts in the public sector.

5.31 From the private sector partner's point of view, the arrangement will only be successful to the extent that it gains a reasonable return on its investment (and perhaps also enhanced political influence).

Chapter summary

- Public sector organisations include: central government departments, local government authorities, QUANGOs, public corporations and municipal enterprises.
- Public sector funding ultimately derives from taxpayers. Funding is used to deliver essential public services, to encourage development, and to pursue socio-economic goals.
- The private and public sectors differ in factors such as ownership, funding, primary objective, competition and stakeholder constituency. This creates some differences in purchasing objectives and constraints – although these should not be overemphasised.
- All areas of the public sector are under pressure to achieve efficiency savings from procurement.
- The activities of procurement in the public sector are more tightly regulated than in the private sector.
- The EU procurement directives aim to foster competition as a stimulus to efficiency in public sector service provision.
- The objectives of public sector organisations differ from those of the private sector. In particular, the priority for the public sector is the achievement of defined service levels rather than the pursuit of profit.

Self-test questions

Numbers in brackets refer to the paragraphs where you can check your answers.

1   List different types of public sector organisation. (1.1)

2   What are the primary objectives of public sector organisations? (1.6)

3   Why do areas of difference between private sector and public sector procurement not necessarily lead to differences in operational procedures? (2.3)

4   List some such areas of difference. (Table 2.1)

5   How does the OGC impact on procurement in central government? (3.3)

6   Describe the main impacts of regulation on public procurement. (4.4)

7   What are the objectives of the EU procurement directives? (4.7)

8   The stakeholders in a public sector organisation are typically less diverse than in a private sector organisation. True or false? (5.2)

9   List some of the distinctive challenges of public sector procurement. (5.5)

10   What are the potential disadvantages of compulsory competitive tendering? (5.14)

11   List methods of achieving value for money in public procurement. (5.27)

12   List (a) advantages and (b) disadvantages claimed for public private partnerships. (5.29, 5.30)

CHAPTER 3

Types of Competitive Markets

Assessment criteria and indicative content

2.1 Explain the implications of different types of competitive markets on procurement and supply

- Defining markets
- Perfect competition, imperfect, oligopolistic, duopolistic and monopolistic markets
- The impact of market competition on the procurement of supplies and services

3.1 Use analytical tools to explain the impact of the external environment on procurement and supply

- The Five Forces Model

Section headings

1. Defining markets
2. Perfect competition
3. Monopoly
4. Monopolistic (imperfect) competition
5. Oligopoly
6. The impact of market competition
7. International markets

Introduction

In this chapter, we introduce another element of the purchasing environment: markets. Markets are the 'places' where buyers and sellers of a product or service are brought together to interact. We'll explain what we mean by 'places' first.

We then go on to consider another important aspect of markets: competition. Buyer spending power (and therefore demand) and production resources (and therefore supply) are limited, so if there is more than one buyer or seller in a market, they will have to compete for a share of the value available. Different market conditions create different types and degrees of competition: from perfect competition at one end of the scale to no competition at all (monopoly) at the other, with imperfect competition in between. We will explore each option in detail.

Finally, we examine the forces that influence the amount and intensity of competition in an industry, using a well known framework: Porter's Five Forces Model. And we add some brief comments on international markets, in preparation for considering the international dimensions of environmental factors, in subsequent chapters.

1 Defining markets

The marketer's perspective and the economist's perspective

1.1 Marketing guru Philip Kotler defines a market as 'the set of actual and potential buyers of a product. These buyers share a particular need or want that can be satisfied through exchange. Thus, the size of a market depends on the number of people who exhibit the need, have resources to engage in exchange, and are willing to offer these resources in exchange for what they want'.

1.2 It is easy to understand a market as a physical location where sellers and potential buyers gather together. And in origin that is exactly what the term denoted. Nowadays, of course, the activities of buying and selling are not necessarily carried out face to face.

1.3 For example, many sellers in consumer markets make their products available through mail order, or by online ordering. In industrial markets too, buyers and sellers do not normally come together in the same physical location. A buyer will make his requirements known by letter, or email, or telephone, by an invitation to tender, or by any of the means provided by market technology. The seller will often supply the need by delivering from a remote location.

1.4 All of this means that the concept of a market is no longer restricted to its original meaning of a physical location. But the more general modern interpretation – a market as a group of buyers potentially willing to exchange resources in order to acquire supplies from sellers – is still valuable.

1.5 Kotler was writing from a marketer's perspective. From this viewpoint it makes sense to define a market as a collection of potential buyers. A marketer naturally views his market as the people who may potentially purchase his products or services. Economists, though, tend to speak of a market as a combined collection of potential buyers and potential sellers. It is this wider concept that we will be examining in the rest of this chapter.

Market structure

1.6 The term 'market structure' refers to different *forms of competition* that might be found in a market. Customer spending power (in product markets) and resources or factors of production (in factor markets) are inevitably limited. This means that if there is more than one player in a market, they will have to compete for a share of the market. The nature and intensity of that competition will influence the behaviour and performance of the players in the market – and their purchasing strategies.

1.7 There are four basic market structures.

- **Perfect competition** is a theoretical construct, which is never really achieved in practice – but is useful for analysing the effects of competition. It represents a set of conditions in which no supplier (among many) has the market power to influence the price of a good: there will be only one price for the good, determined by total market supply and demand.
- **Monopoly** is another theoretical construct at the opposite end of the scale: a situation in which no competition exists at all, because a single producer supplies the whole market. This producer has ultimate market power, and can (unless regulated) decide what it will charge for the good.

- **Monopolistic competition** is a form of 'imperfect' competition. It describes a situation where there is competition between a large number of suppliers producing goods which are slightly different (or differentiated) in some way: in specification, or packaging, or consumer perception, say. These differences may allow suppliers to set slightly varying prices for a good.
- **Oligopoly** is another form of 'imperfect' competition. It describes a situation where there is competition between a small number of large suppliers of differentiated goods. Such suppliers have considerable market power to set prices, but will be reluctant to engage in unilateral price rises (risk of losing market share) or cuts (risk of creating a price war): instead, they will usually work together to keep prices stable.

1.8 These structures can be seen as a continuum from very competitive markets to markets in which there is no competition at all: Figure 3.1.

Figure 3.1 *The competitive spectrum*

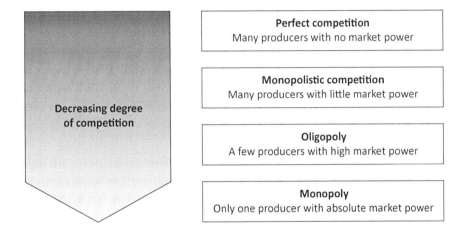

2   Perfect competition

Market conditions creating a perfectly competitive market

2.1 Perfect competition is an 'ideal' situation in which no player in the market has market power to influence the price of a good. The market conditions which need to be fulfilled to bring this situation about are as follows.

- There are many buyers and sellers: each is so small relative to the total market that its actions cannot affect the market. For example, there is no buyer able to buy such large quantities that it could influence the market price.
- The goods being marketed are 'homogeneous': in other words, identical.
- 'Perfect information' about the market is available to all parties.
- There is no 'economic friction': the same market factors (eg risk, storage and transport costs) affect all parties equally.
- There are no 'barriers to entry or exit': firms can choose to enter or leave the market without cost. (We will discuss this further below.)
- There is 'perfect mobility': producers can use resources for any purpose, and consumers can purchase from any supplier, without incurring switching costs.

2.2 What this essentially means is that no supplier or buyer will have power to influence the price of the good in the market. If one supplier tries to charge a higher price than the others, everyone will know (because of perfect information) – and there will be no barrier to consumers simply switching to another supplier (because the goods are identical and all other factors are equal). All firms will have to toe the line of market price, which will be determined by supply and demand in the total market: they are said to be *price takers* – accepting the 'going rate' for the good.

2.3 Market price will generally settle at a level which allows suppliers to make 'normal profits': that is, sufficient revenue to cover their costs, plus a margin of profit sufficient for them to stay in business. If a firm earns less than this, in the absence of barriers to exit, it will simply leave the market. If a firm earns more than this ('abnormal profits'), everyone will know: in the absence of barriers to entry, other firms will enter the market seeking to share in the supra-normal profits that are available – and with more competition and higher supply, prices will fall, returning profits to the normal level.

Barriers to entry and exit

2.4 *Barriers to entry* are factors which reduce the attractiveness or profitability of a market to potential new competitors from outside, and therefore reduce the likelihood that they will enter the market. In perfect competition, no such barriers exist – but in oligopoly and monopoly markets, firms will have an interest in *erecting* such barriers (if they do not already exist) in order to protect their power and profits.

2.5 The main barriers to entry include the following.

- Economies of scale and other cost advantages for established competitors (eg bulk purchasing and production economies, fewer marketing costs, no learning curve, preferential access to necessary inputs), allowing them to squeeze out new entrants with a price war if necessary
- High capital investment requirements in order to enter the market
- Product differentiation and brand identity: hard-to-imitate offerings with costly-to-counter market profile and customer loyalty. Established competitors can afford to spend heavily on advertising, the cost of which will be spread over a large number of units sold: newer, smaller entrants may struggle to advertise at levels required to create awareness and woo customers from existing players.
- Switching costs (eg time, inconvenience, unfamiliarity with the new product, perhaps cost of getting out of existing contracts) and customer loyalty to existing brands, hindering new product trial and adoption by the market
- Existing players' control over supply and distribution channels (perhaps on a selective or exclusive basis which would hinder competitors)
- Existing players' control over a natural resource for which no close substitutes exist (eg ownership of or access to minerals or forests)
- Restricted labour or skill supply (eg the provision of accountancy and legal services being restricted to members of appropriate professional bodies)
- Government policy and legislative barriers: for example, laws protecting established players' intellectual property (eg design patents and copyrights) or physical property (such as mineral or fishing rights).

2.6 *Barriers to exit* are factors which make it difficult for an existing supplier to *leave* an industry, if it proves unattractive or unprofitable. Here are some barriers to exit.

- A lack of assets with significant break-up, re-sale or re-use value, so that the firm will not be able to realise any value from them (other than by continuing to use them)
- The cost of redundancy payments, if workers have to be laid off as a result of the closure or

change of activity

- Effects on other divisions or activities maintained by the firm: loss of morale and/or strategic direction due to the divestment, loss of complementary products (which may have an impact on the sale of other items in the product range), loss of managerial talent (if not transferred to other divisions)
- Reputational damage, as a result of factory closures, product withdrawals and so on – which may impact on the firm's other product lines
- Corporate social responsibility and/or government pressure to maintain employment and the production of essential goods and services (even if they are unprofitable).

Are there any perfectly competitive markets?

2.7   There are some markets which arguably come close to being perfectly competitive. The stock markets and foreign exchange markets are examples: there are many operators in the market; each company's shares and each country's currency are identical; there is an emphasis on transparency and information is transmitted very quickly to all market participants; and transaction costs are similar for all operators. However, some operators (eg large pension funds or insurance companies) do have market power; and there are barriers to entry (eg in the form of minimum authorised share capital).

The implications of perfect competition for procurement

2.8   Perfect competition means that there will be literally nothing to choose between one supplier and another. Buyers have perfect information about all suppliers' prices, and since all offerings are identical, they are perfectly free to switch suppliers to secure the market rate: any supplier who charges above the market price, or seeks abnormal profit margins, will quickly have to come into line in order to stay competitive. Buyers may also seek to play suppliers against each other to secure prices below market rate: it doesn't matter if a supplier is driven out of business, because there are plenty of others – and no costs of exit for the supplier.

2.9   Even where a market is slightly less than perfect, there will be the same incentive for suppliers to compete on price, and this will be to buyers' advantage: given identical offerings, and low switching costs, buyers have the market power to 'shop around'.

2.10   From the buyer's viewpoint, the *downside* of perfect competition is that there may be many buyers as well as many sellers. Small buyers will lack market power to influence suppliers on price: if they don't like the terms of business, suppliers will know they can sell their goods to plenty of other buyers instead.

3   Monopoly

Features of a monopoly

3.1   In its 'ideal' form, a monopoly exists when one producer supplies the whole market. The conditions for a monopoly are as follows.

- Only one supplier of the good exists. It may be a single organisation, or a group of producers acting together to control supply (eg a cartel such as the Organisation of Petroleum Exporting Countries, or OPEC).
- There are barriers to entry, preventing other firms from entering the market (eg high set-up

costs, high customer loyalty to the existing producer, or the existing producer monopolising sources of supply and distribution channels).

- There are no close substitutes for the good being produced (which would enable buyers to switch).

3.2 If these conditions are met, the monopolist essentially controls supply, and has absolute power to determine the price of the good in its market: it is said to be a *price maker*. It is this feature which can lead to consumers being over-charged, which is why monopoly markets are usually regulated, as we will see.

3.3 Control over supply and price enables monopolists to achieve and sustain abnormal profits, because there are no competitors to increase supply (lowering prices and therefore eroding profits).

Price discrimination

3.4 A monopolist may be able to operate *price discrimination:* charging different prices for the same good in different markets or market segments. So, for example, the same train ticket may be more expensive in peak commuter hours than in off-peak hours – or if booked in person rather than online. Consumers with higher disposable income will be willing to pay more for the same good or service than less affluent consumers (perhaps even perceiving that the higher price tag means better quality).

3.5 In order for price discrimination to be possible, the firm must be able to identify different market segments with different demand conditions, so that different prices are tolerated by each. The higher price will be charged to the market where the demand is relatively 'inelastic' (that is, where demand is not sensitive to price changes) and the lower price where it is relatively 'elastic' (where demand is sensitive to price). There must also be no possibility of resale by one consumer to another, so people charged the lower price can't go out and resell the good to those being charged the higher price, possibly undercutting the original provider.

3.6 You might think of price discrimination as 'discriminatory' in a bad sense, exploiting some consumers by charging them more for the same good. However, it has some benefits for both the supplier and the consumer.

- It allows efficient resource usage: lower prices can be used to stimulate sales in 'off-peak' periods, to shift unused stock (or fill last-minute vacancies) – and hence to smooth out fluctuations in demand.
- It takes into account affordability for different groups of consumers, allowing less affluent groups equal access to goods and services, and charging more to groups who are able and willing to pay more.

Regulation of monopoly

3.7 UK law defines a monopoly, for the purposes of regulation, as a situation in which one firm or group of firms acting together (a cartel) supplies or purchases 25% or more of all goods or services of a particular type in the UK, or in a part of the UK. This is obviously not a *pure* monopoly, but represents considerable power to dictate terms in a market.

3.8 UK legislation (including the Competition Act 1998 and Fair Trading Act 1973) is designed to regulate monopolies – and mergers which would result in monopolies – in the public interest. A monopoly may be considered to endanger the public interest if its effect is: to hinder effective competition; to damage consumer interests (eg by unfairly raising prices or reducing quality); to limit development; or to distort the distribution of industry and employment. If the Office of Fair Trading finds evidence of harmful conduct by a monopoly, it may seek assurances that the organisation(s) will alter anti-competitive business practices – or may refer the matter to the Competition Commission.

3.9 Similar provisions apply in European law: Article 82 of the Treaty of Rome prohibits abuse of a monopoly position by an organisation within the EU. In this case a 'monopoly position' is defined not in terms of market share, but relative economic strength: the ability of a company to 'behave to an appreciable extent independently of its competitors, customers and ultimately of its consumers'. Software giant Microsoft, for example, has been repeatedly investigated (and fined) by the European Commission for abusing its dominant market position to freeze out competing products.

3.10 So is there such a thing as a pure monopoly? Perhaps the purest examples of monopoly in the UK were the old nationalised utilities like British Gas – but they have now been privatised, and the market is open to competition (although it has been slow to develop, with significant barriers to entry).

The implications of monopoly for procurement

3.11 The main concern for buyers will be a *monopoly supplier*'s absolute power in the market: there will be no opportunity for the buyer to take its business elsewhere, so the monopolist will be able to dictate terms and conditions of trade. The only alternatives will be to seek substitute goods or services which would serve the same purpose, *or* to seek new supply markets, perhaps internationally: this may even be a helpful spur to strategic thinking and innovation!

3.12 Prices will generally be higher in the absence of competition, and the buyer will not be able to exert pressure to reduce prices – nor to improve quality or service levels: its business is likely to represent only a small part of the supplier's revenue. However, monopolists enjoy *economies of scale:* that is, cost savings due to their large size. Large-scale operations make greater use of advanced machinery and efficient mass production techniques; are able to access finance more cheaply; are able to benefit from bulk discounts on purchases; and so on. Some of these cost savings *may* be passed on to buyers in the form of reasonable prices – although this may have to be achieved by regulation. Regulation limits the prices that monopolists are allowed to charge, in the case of privatised industries in the UK, for example.

3.13 Another issue of concern is that buyers may be unable to specify their exact supply requirements, since the monopoly supplier has little incentive to tailor its product range to the needs of a large number of potential buyers. There may be little or no choice, customisation or innovation – and this might be a serious problem for buyers whose own competitive market is highly specialised or fast-changing. Again, however, this is not *necessarily* the case: monopolists may have more resources to invest in customisation, flexibility and innovation, with the incentive of even higher profits.

3.14 You should also be able to think of the issues raised by the reverse set of circumstances: the position of suppliers faced with a *monopoly buyer,* with absolute bargaining power. There will be considerable risk for suppliers forced to adapt their technology, processes and offerings to the needs of a single customer: if they lose the monopoly's custom, there may be few immediate alternative markets. Suppliers may be driven out of business when large customers, on whom they are highly dependent, squeeze their prices beyond the point of sustainability, or terminate the supply relationship.

4   Monopolistic (imperfect) competition

Features of monopolistic competition

4.1   'Monopolistic competition' is not to be confused with 'monopoly'. It is a form of imperfect competition, brought about where the following market conditions apply.

- There are many suppliers (though not as many as in perfect competition)
- Goods are *not* homogeneous: each supplier produces a good which is slightly differentiated from its competitors. (This means that each supplier is a monopoly for its own 'version' of a good – hence 'monopolistic' – but faces competition in the market for the good in general. Apple is a monopoly producer of iPods, but there are many types of MP3 players on the market.)
- There are barriers to entry (such as customer loyalty and brand strength), but not sufficient to prevent other firms from entering the market in the long term.

4.2   Products may be different in their technical specifications or performance, or differentiation may be added to the total offering: better after-sales service, say, or longer warranty periods. The difference may also lie in the perception of consumers, rather than in the product itself: product 'positioning' is the name given in marketing to consumers' perception of a product's values and attributes in comparison to competitors. Consumers can be encouraged to develop a preference for, and ultimately a loyalty to, a product through distinctive branding, packaging and promotion – even if the product itself is identical to its competitors. (Why is an iPod different from another functionally similar MP3 player, for example?)

4.3   Differentiation gives firms a degree of market power, as (unlike in a perfectly competitive market, where goods are identical) consumers may develop a preference for certain features and products, allowing suppliers to charge a little above market price without losing all their customers. In fact, it may be possible to *increase* demand for a product by raising prices slightly, where consumers perceive this to be a sign of high-quality or high-status goods. Similarly, a firm which lowers its prices slightly will not necessarily benefit from increased demand, because many consumers will remain loyal to their preferred brand.

4.4   With the ability to sustain slightly above-market prices, firms may be able to make modest super-normal profits in the short term – although in the long run, super-normal profits will still attract new competitors, which will bring profits back into line.

4.5   It could be argued that imperfect competition is wasteful of resources, compared to perfect competition, because of the investment in promotion and other forms of differentiation. However, this can be seen as the price society has to pay for choice.

4.6   Monopolistic competition is very common: you should be able to think of many examples, from clothes to cereals to cars.

Implications of monopolistic competition for procurement

4.7 These are probably the market conditions you will face most commonly in your professional work as a purchaser. They create a more complicated market than either of the theoretical extremes, in that suppliers will compete along a range of different dimensions: not just price, but non-price criteria such as quality, variety, flexibility, speed of delivery, service and so on. Buyers will need to have a clear idea of what price and non-price criteria are most important for a given purchase category in a given set of circumstances, in order to select the right suppliers for their needs.

4.8 The balance of power between buyers and sellers will also be more complex: buyers will have the power to switch brands, but not without cost (researching other suitable suppliers, losing their 'preferred' brand and so on). There may be room for negotiation of mutually satisfying purchase contracts and relationships, achieving a balance between the needs of both sides.

5 Oligopoly

Features of oligopoly

5.1 An oligopoly is a situation in which a small number of large producers dominate a market in which products are differentiated. This may sound like monopolistic competition, only with fewer players – but the number of players makes a significant difference. With so few firms in the market, each having a significant share of the total market, actions by any one will have direct consequences for all the others. No firm in the market can take decisions independently of the others, because of the likelihood that competitors will respond. (You may sometimes meet references to an oligopoly where the suppliers are just two in number: a **duopoly**.)

5.2 This creates a distinctive tactical climate.

- There is little *price competition* in the market. Firms have similar market knowledge, so their cost structures and prices will be broadly similar. Moreover, a firm will be reluctant to lower prices unilaterally, because competitors will simply do the same to protect their market share – creating price wars in which the whole industry will lose out. And it will be reluctant to *raise* prices unilaterally, because if competitors *don't* do the same, it may lose market share.
- Competition often takes *non-price forms*: product differentiation supported by branding, advertising, promotions (special offers) and added-value benefits (eg sales and after-sales service, loyalty reward programmes and so on). Think about how the major supermarket or petrol station chains try to stimulate sales and customer loyalty, for example.
- Market prices tend to be set by non-competitive means, in order to maintain price stability and avoid damaging price wars. One approach is that a dominant firm takes the lead in setting the market price, and smaller firms follow suit: this is called *price leadership.* Another approach is for firms in the market to agree between them what prices will be: this is called 'collusion'. (We will discuss it further below.)
- Firms often maintain high barriers to new competitors entering the market, in order to preserve the *status quo* and their market share: for example, by strong branding, controlling channels of supply and distribution, and preventing newcomers from joining cartels.

5.3 Oligopolists have a great deal of market power, by virtue of their size. Super-normal profits are therefore achievable, depending on the strength of competitors and the level of prices that are sustainable in the market.

5.4 There are many examples of oligopoly markets, including the tobacco, brewing, confectionery and toy industries – in all of which, the top few firms in the industry have a market share over 85%.

Collusion in oligopoly markets

5.5 There is a temptation for the few firms in an oligopolistic market to join forces to keep out new competitors and fix prices. This can be done by various forms of collusion.

5.6 A **price cartel** or **price ring** is formed when a group of oligopoly firms join forces to agree – and therefore control – output quotas (the amount that will be produced) and market prices. Each participant can increase its profits, if all major competitors charge the same price: potentially, the same price as a monopoly might be able to charge.

5.7 In order for a cartel to be successful, it must include most or all of the major producers and distributors (in order to avoid price competition). There must not be close substitutes for the product (in order to avoid customers' switching in response to high prices), and demand cannot be too price sensitive (so that demand will not fall so much, in response to high prices, that the producers' income will be reduced rather than raised). In addition, the participants must be able to agree on their share of the total supply to the market (which dictates their proportion of the revenue and profits available): this is sometimes the hardest hurdle of all.

5.8 The best known cartel is OPEC, which controls most of the oil production in the world. However, EU treaty provisions, the UK Competition Act and the Enterprise Act 2002 now outlaw cartels. In a well-known 2003 case, for example, a group of ten businesses was found to have illegally entered price-fixing agreements in relation to the sale of replica football kit, around the time of the Euro 2000 Championship (the 'duplicate kit cartel').

5.9 There are also various forms of *informal price collusion*, including the following.

- Systems of 'recommended retail prices', with sellers discouraged from selling at lower or differentiated prices.
- Price leadership by one firm, which is then followed by others in the market.

5.10 Informal collusion is also outlawed in most countries, because its effect is to reduce or distort competition between firms, to the detriment of consumers. Even so, it goes on: collusion includes not just explicit agreements but implicit 'understandings' and even competitors watching each others' pricing decisions and following suit. These kinds of behaviour can be difficult to control.

5.11 Apart from collusive agreements being against the best interests of the consumer, and subject to law and public scrutiny (with the risk of financial penalties and reputational damage), they are also tricky for the participants. This is because of the temptation for cartel members to break ranks for short-term profit-taking. Nevertheless, the market is best served in the long run by price stability, so competition is usually focused on non-price differentiation and promotion.

Implications of oligopoly for procurement

5.12 Because of the non-homogeneity of goods in the market, buyers will (as with monopolistic competition) have a degree of product choice. Because of the oligopoly's avoidance of price competition, particular emphasis will have to be placed on getting the best possible value for money through a combination of non-price factors: if buyers cannot negotiate on price, they will need to use whatever buyer power they have to secure the best possible service, support and other added value benefits.

5.13 In an oligopoly supply market, suppliers have strong market power by virtue of their size and small number – and any type of formal or informal collusion will add to their bargaining strength and reduce that of buyers. As with a monopoly, oligopoly suppliers can therefore charge high prices – but will benefit from economies of scale which they *may* choose to pass on to buyers. Buyers may seek to enhance their bargaining power in various ways: by developing their negotiating skills; perhaps by consolidating their purchases; or by banding together in a buying consortium with other purchasing organisations, so that they can offer a larger volume of business to a given supplier.

5.14 For a supplier dealing with an oligopoly *buyer*, the position will be reversed. The buyer will represent a potentially large volume of business (although it may divide its demand among a large number of suppliers), allowing the supplier economies of scale and standardisation. On the other hand, bargaining power will lie with the buyer, enabling it to force prices down and raise quality and service (in the interests of its own competitive advantage).

Round-up of market structures

5.15 Here is a summary and comparison of the key features of the four market structures: Table 3.1.

Table 3.1 *Comparison of market structures*

PERFECT COMPETITION	MONOPOLISTIC COMPETITION	OLIGOPOLY	MONOPOLY
Very many small suppliers	Many slightly larger suppliers	Few large suppliers	One supplier
No market power	Little market power	High market power	Absolute market power
Homogeneous goods: suppliers' products are interchangeable	Differentiated goods: suppliers' products are close substitutes	Differentiated goods: degree of substitution variable	No substitutes
One market price: suppliers are 'price takers'	Price competition	Seeking of price stability by price leadership or collusion	Price set by one 'price maker': potential for price discrimination
Normal profits	Small abnormal profits, short term	Abnormal profits, depending on competition	Abnormal profits
No advertising or branding (everyone knows all goods identical)	Heavy advertising and branding > differentiation	Much advertising and branding > non-price competition	Not much advertising or branding required (no competition)
No barriers to entry	No barriers to entry in the long run	Barriers to entry	Barriers to entry

6 The impact of market competition

6.1 Some of the key texts on competition and competitive advantage were written in the 1980s by Professor Michael Porter. He suggested that 'competition in an industry is rooted in its underlying economics' (as we have already seen) and that 'competitive forces exist that go well beyond the established combatants in a particular industry'. Porter developed a framework which argues that the extent of competition in an industry – and therefore its attractiveness or potential profitability to any given player within it – depends on the interaction of five forces in the organisation's industry environment.

Porter's Five Forces Model

6.2 Although the *five forces model,* as it is called, is not mentioned explicitly in your syllabus, it is an important tool for understanding markets. We will therefore summarise its main features here.

6.3 Five forces determine the extent of competition in an industry: Figure 3.2.

Figure 3.2 *Porter's five forces model*

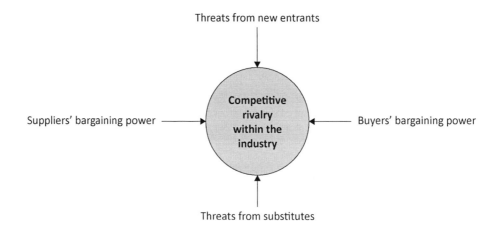

6.4 **Potential new entrants** to an industry may make it more competitive by: expanding supply (without necessarily increasing market demand); striving to penetrate the market and build market share, perhaps by innovating or competing aggressively; and increasing costs, as they bid for factors of production. It is therefore in the interests of existing competitors to deter new entrants. The strength of the threat from new entrants will vary from industry to industry, according to the strength of barriers to entry (discussed earlier) – and the response of existing competitors to any new entrant. (If existing players typically respond to new competitors by competing aggressively on price, a prospective entrant might think twice about whether entry will be profitable...)

6.5 **Substitute products** are alternative products that serve the same purpose (eg postal services, courier services, fax machines, e-mail), making it easy for buyers to switch, and therefore limiting the price that a company can charge for its products. There is a particular risk in that a company may not see a substitute coming, if it results from innovation. Where there are plenty of substitutes available, demand for a product is likely to be relatively price sensitive: buyers are more likely to switch in response to price rises (or price cuts by competitors). Improved price or value positioning in substitute products is therefore a significant threat.

6.6 **Buyer power** may make an industry more competitive by enabling buyers (customers) to: force down prices; bargain for higher quality or improved services; or play competing providers against each other. Porter suggested that buyers are particularly powerful in the following situations.

- They are limited in number and/or large in size, relative to supplying firms.
- Their spend is a high proportion of suppliers' revenue (but not a high proportion of their own spend, since this will make them dependent on the supplier).
- Products/services are undifferentiated, or there are substitute products, making it easy to switch suppliers.
- There is potential for 'backward integration' (ie buyers can own or control their suppliers: a book publisher taking over a printing company, say).

6.7 **Supplier power** (as we saw in the case of oligopolists and monopolists) is generally exercised to raise prices, squeezing buyers' profits (especially if they are unable to recover their cost increases by raising their own prices). Suppliers are particularly powerful in the following situations.

- They are limited in number and/or large in size, relative to buying firms.
- There are few substitute products and/or the supplier's product (and/or service) is highly differentiated.
- The volume purchased by the buyer or industry is not important to the supplier.
- The supplier's product is an important component in the buyer's business.
- The switching cost for buyers is high (eg because of investment in the relationship with a particular supplier, or contract penalties for switching).
- There is potential for 'forward integration' (ie suppliers can own or control their buyers: a clothing manufacturer opening retail stores, say).

6.8 The **intensity of rivalry** among current competitors may range, as we have seen, from collusion between competitors (in order to maintain and share the profits available in the industry) to the other extreme of aggressive competitive strategies such as innovation, price wars and promotional battles, where one firm's gain is another firm's loss. Rivalry is likely to be more intense in the following situations.

- There are many equally-balanced competitors.
- There is a slow rate of industry growth. (If the 'pie' isn't getting larger, the only way firms can grow will be to compete for a bigger 'slice'.)
- There is a lack of product and service differentiation.
- There are high fixed costs of production, since firms need higher revenue to cover them and make a profit.
- There are high barriers to exit, so it is less costly to compete harder than to withdraw from the industry.

6.9 You might like to think about the mobile phone industry, for example, or the soft drinks industry (the famous 'Cola wars' between Pepsi and Coke). What makes competition in these industries so intense – and on what basis do the major players seek to compete (a) with potential new entrants and (b) with each other?

Industry structure

6.10 Porter also classified industry structures according to the amount and type of competition within them.

- **Fragmented industries** are 'populated by a large number of small and medium-sized companies' and characterised by 'the absence of market leaders with the power to shape industry events'. You should be able to see how this corresponds to the market structure of perfect or monopolistic competition. An example of a fragmented industry in the UK might be hairdressing (since there are few large chains of salons).
- **Concentrated industries** are dominated by a small number of large competitors, which are able to exercise a significant influence over the market. You should be able to see how this corresponds to the market structure of oligopoly.

6.11 Industries may become fragmented over time, if their markets are attractive to smaller firms. This may be the case if barriers to entry are low, or there are few economies of scale to be exploited by larger firms; if innovation and flexibility are required in response to changing or fluctuating demand; if 'local' contacts, differentiation and reputation are important; or if the market itself is fragmented into small segments of customers with distinct tastes or needs (separate niche markets not worth the while of a large organisation to pursue). You might like to think about which of these conditions apply to the increasing fragmentation of the media and publishing industry, for example, with the availability of satellite and digital TV, web-based publishing and so on.

6.12 On the other hand, industries may become (or remain) concentrated, if conditions favour fewer, larger players: there are high barriers to entry, high costs of staying in business and competing, and/or good economies of scale available (where it is cheaper to purchase, produce, distribute and market goods in bulk). There may be consolidation of smaller competitors into fewer, larger ones, through mergers and acquisitions (although the larger resulting groups or chains may retain the distinctive features and markets of their component parts, eg by retaining different brands). A standardised product or service offering may become preferred to smaller, more customised competitors, enabling customers' needs to be fulfilled by fewer firms: think about large fast food chains and supermarkets, for example.

6.13 Porter also noted the existence of **emerging industries**: new or re-formed industries which have not yet settled into established patterns of competition. These may be created by technological innovation (eg creating electronic publishing and music industries) or social change (eg creating eco-friendly industries such as reverse logistics, and waste storage and recycling).

6.14 Emerging industries pose distinctive problems for organisations active within them, because of early barriers to entry (technology development, access to materials, problems obtaining funding, problems establishing a market) and uncertainty about the market and competition. Internal capabilities may have to be developed (including purchasing, in contexts where supply markets may not yet be established) and external environmental factors may be unfamiliar.

6.15 Emerging markets may also require a different approach to competition. If a company is first into an emerging market (eg discovering and patenting a new technology), it may choose *not* to maintain barriers to entry, in order to establish a monopoly, but to *encourage* competition (eg by licensing the technology to competitors), in order to co-opt other firms in building the profile and size of the market.

Monitoring competitors

6.16 Competitors are an important part of the external micro (market and industry) environment of purchasing.

- An organisation's strategies and products will, to an extent, be influenced by the need to gain or maintain an advantage over competitors in the market. Managers will attempt to predict what competitors will do, in order proactively to counter threats (or exploit opportunities) arising from their plans. So, for example, purchasers may need to monitor competitors' materials costs and quality, in order for their own purchasing and products to stay competitive.
- Competitors may be used as benchmarks for key competencies that are valued by the market. The organisation may measure its customer service, quality management or procurement efficiency, say, against the standards set by key competitors or market leaders.
- Competitors may seek advantage by controlling supply and distribution channels, eg by forming preferential relationships with suppliers or distributors, or negotiating exclusive supply and distribution contracts. An organisation's purchasers are therefore in direct competition with competitors' purchasers, especially where supplies are limited or scarce.

6.17 **Competitor analysis** is therefore a key component of environmental analysis. It involves analysing competitors' goals, capabilities (strengths and weaknesses), strategies (on what basis is it aiming to compete: price, product differentiation, niche markets?) and likely response to environmental threats and opportunities. Purchasers may, for example, need to look at competitors' relationships with key suppliers; whether they have (or may be able to obtain) control over sources of key or scarce supplies; how well they are able to control or reduce purchasing costs (enabling greater profitability and/or price competition); and so on.

7 International markets

Why trade internationally?

7.1 It should be obvious that markets – places where buyers and sellers interact – can be international as well as local or national. Even if a firm does not operate in an international *product* market (ie producing goods for export to other countries), it is quite likely, these days, to operate in an international *supply* market (ie purchasing and importing supplies from other countries).

7.2 We can consider the growth of international trade from two viewpoints: the viewpoint of a country as a whole (a macro-economic viewpoint), and the viewpoint of an individual firm (or purchasing department).

7.3 *Countries* involve themselves in international trade for two main reasons.

- Countries differ in the natural resources they control and the areas of skill and expertise they have developed. Like individual people, countries can benefit from their differences by reaching agreement that each will do whatever it does best and provide what it can produce most efficiently. A country which does not have oil, say, is obliged to buy from a country which has a surplus of oil for export. A country with high labour costs may import manufactured goods from countries such as China which have the capacity to produce them at lower cost.
- If countries can specialise (to an extent) in the production of certain goods or the provision of certain services, it may be able to produce them on a larger scale – and thus benefit from economies of scale. The Japanese domination of the market in electronic goods in recent years is one example of this effect. International trade enables different countries to reap the benefits of specialisation, while still ensuring that a variety of goods and services is available.

7.4 The theory that international trade is for the mutual benefit of the partners involved is known as the **theory of comparative advantage.** A country can increase its national income – and potentially improve the standard of living of its population – by specialising in the manufacture of those products, or provision of those services, in which it has the highest productivity or comparative advantage over other nations. (Think about the transformation of the Indian economy, as a result of specialisation in call centre services, say, supported by global ICT links.) Because each nation is able to use its resources to best effect, and nations effectively 'pool' their best resources, the theory suggests that the overall result of international trade is to raise overall economic prosperity and well-being.

7.5 Other advantages are claimed for international trade.

- The stimulation of local economic activity helps to create employment, leading to greater prosperity, educational development and other standard-of-living benefits. Smaller developing nations particularly benefit from the wider scope of markets, since their domestic economy may have represented too small a market to allow development and resulting economies of scale.

- The siting of operations in developing countries may bring investment in technology, infrastructure, education and skill development which the host country could not afford on its own. It may also bring about improvements in human rights and labour conditions, whenever foreign investors and buyers operate ethical (CSR) policies and monitoring.
- Global consumers benefit from more choice of products and services and competitive pricing.
- It has been argued that international trade is a primary mechanism for positive international relations and a deterrent to conflict.

7.6 *Individual firms* may wish to enter international product or supply markets for any of the following reasons.

- The domestic market is mature or 'saturated' with their products, with no room for growth, so they need to open up new markets overseas, to maintain sales growth (or, it is sometimes argued, to offload stock which has become obsolete in the domestic market).
- Particular materials or resources are not available (or have become scarce and costly) in the domestic supply market.
- Domestic suppliers have become complacent or uncompetitive on price, compared to overseas suppliers (who may have readier access to resources, lower labour costs or less stringent regulatory regimes): one of the main reasons for international sourcing is its potential cost savings.
- Exchange rates support the exporting of domestically produced goods (by making their price competitive in the overseas market) or the importing of overseas-produced supplies (by making their price competitive with the domestic supply market). We will explain how this works in Chapter 6.
- Technological advances, particularly in information and communication technology, reduces the cost and risk of sourcing internationally: it is easier to gather information, monitor and manage suppliers, track deliveries and so on.

Barriers to international trade

7.7 Now for the downside: the reasons why not every company markets or sources internationally – and why the decision to source internationally (of most relevance to purchasers) must be taken with care.

- Costs of identifying, evaluating and developing new product and supply markets, in situations where information may be difficult to obtain
- Differences in culture, legal systems and infrastructure development, which may cause incompatibility, misunderstanding or conflict. (On the marketing side, consumers may have different perceptions, tastes and values, and may not have access to a wide range of advertising media. On the supply side, suppliers may have different technical, quality or ethical standards, for example.)
- Differences in language and resulting costs of translation (and risks of mis-translation. There are some very funny examples of brand names translating badly: like the Vauxhall Nova car – 'No va' meaning 'doesn't go' in Spanish.)
- Transport risks, costs and delays, caused by distance and infrastructure differences
- Currency management issues and exchange rate risk
- Market risks, posed by factors such as political instability or policy change, industrial unrest or natural factors (eg drought or flood)

7.8 In addition, governments may place restrictions on international trade, in order to protect their country's producers from competition from imports: a policy called 'protectionism'. Such restrictions include: import quotas (limiting the volume of specified goods allowed into the country); tariffs (taxes placed on imported goods); and subsidies to domestic producers (to make them more competitive).

7.9 Although the trend is now to reduce trade restrictions, they can perform a useful function: protecting strategic industries (in order to preserve the economies which depend on them); protecting emerging industries (in order to encourage development); and improving a country's 'balance of payments' (the ratio of its exports to imports).

Globalisation

7.10 Globalisation may be defined as 'the increasing integration of internationally dispersed economic activity' (Boddy).

7.11 This integration may involve the globalisation of *markets*. It has been argued that with worldwide access to media, travel and communications, there has been a convergence of consumer needs and wants: major brands (such as Coca Cola or McDonald's) can be sold worldwide, without much modification for particular geographic markets. This has opened up new markets and offered economies of scale – but these advantages have proved hard to grasp for some brands, which lost (or failed to gain) market share against locally-adapted brands which catered to specific national and regional cultures, tastes and conditions. (Marks & Spencer, for example, has had a mixed history with its international stores.)

7.12 A parallel development has been the globalisation of *production*. High domestic labour costs, for labour-intensive operations, has enabled intense competition from cheaper imports originating in countries with lower-cost labour. (Think about industries such as electronic goods, clothing, footwear and toy manufacture, for example.) This has stimulated the growth of outsourcing, as developed countries have outsourced the production of finished goods and components, and the delivery of service, to countries such as Taiwan, China, South Korea, Singapore, Sri Lanka and India. The media is now full of examples of companies 'offshoring' their administrative work and telephone enquires (eg major banks) and product assembly (eg Hitachi, Compaq, Mattel).

7.13 The main drivers for any given industry to become globalised (based on Yip, *Total Global Strategy*) include the following: Table 3.2.

Table 3.2 *Drivers for globalisation of an industry*

FACTOR	EXAMPLES
Market factors	• Convergence of customer needs, creating demand for products and services to be available on a worldwide basis • Globalised marketing firms becoming global customers – seeking suppliers who can also operate on a worldwide basis • Transferable marketing, with the development of global communication and distribution channels (including the internet).
Cost factors	• Economies of scale available through the large potential volume of global sales • Sourcing efficiencies, as firms are able to select the lowest-cost supplier from anywhere in the world • Product development costs: where development costs are high, firms will need to extend the earning potential of products by selling into international markets
Government factors	• Trade policies, which have tended to support free markets between nations (reducing protectionist barriers to trade) • Harmonisation of technical standards, which has enabled the sourcing of standardised components, compatible systems etc • Host government policies, aimed at encouraging global operators to base themselves in their countries, eg via tax incentives
Competitive factors	• Companies faced with global competition will have to consider becoming global themselves, in order to stay competitive
Technology factors	Developments in ICT support and enable: • 'Virtual organisation': sourcing expertise and collaboration regardless of location (eg off-shored administrative centres) • Global supply (eg through access to international supply market information, improved supplier management and monitoring) • Global logistics (eg through computerised transport planning and delivery tracking) • General improvements in international business communication (eg through email)

Opposition to globalisation

7.14 The arguments in favour of globalisation are broadly the same as those for international trade in general. However, it should be obvious from TV footage of violent protests outside World Trade Organisation and G8 meetings that there is a contrary viewpoint! Those opposed to globalisation argue as follows.

- It encourages the exploitation of labour in developing nations (poor wages, poor conditions, child labour and so on) for lower-cost production.
- It encourages the exploitation of local markets, using them as dumping grounds for poor-quality or obsolete goods, and leading to increased foreign debt.
- It 'exports' pollution, deforestation, urbanisation and other environmental damage to developing nations.
- It undermines governments in the management of their own domestic economies, particularly through the influence of the World Trade Organisation and the power of global corporations (whose turnover exceeds the total economic output of some nations...)
- It causes unemployment in developed nations, where justified expectations of pay and conditions make labour 'uncompetitive' with cheap-labour competitors.
- It squeezes small, local businesses out of markets, with negative effects on competition, communities and cultures. (There is a well-publicised cultural fight-back by small local retailers against giants like WalMart, for example, and by 'slow food' producers against the McDonald's of the world...)
- It encourages the erosion of local cultures and the loss of local languages.

3

Chapter summary

- A market is a 'place' where buyers and sellers interact. A market economy is one in which economic choices (what to produce, how, for whom and at what price) are made by the market via the market mechanism: supply and demand.
- Demand (the amount of goods consumers want to buy) usually falls as prices rise, in a downward demand curve. Supply (the amount of goods firms want to produce) usually rises as prices rise, in an upward supply curve. The market eventually stabilises at a price where supply equals demand (equilibrium price).
- Market structure refers to different forms and amounts of competition in a market. There are four basic market structures: perfect competition (many producers with no market power); monopolistic competition (many producers with some market power due to differentiation); oligopoly (a few large producers with high market power); and monopoly (only one producer with absolute market power).
- Each market structure depends on particular market conditions (number of suppliers and buyers, homogeneity or differentiation of goods, barriers to entry and so on). Each has particular characteristics: one market price in perfect competition; differentiation in monopolistic competition; competitive tactics and collusion in oligopoly; and absolute market power in monopoly. Each has advantages and/or disadvantages for a purchaser. You should revise these areas in detail.
- Porter's five forces model suggests that the extent of competition in a given industry environment is determined by: potential market entrants (and barriers to entry); substitute products; buyer power; supplier power; and the intensity of rivalry between competing firms.
- There are strong drivers for international trade (in both product and supply markets) and globalisation (the integration of globally dispersed economic activity). However, both are subject to challenges, risks and barriers which marketers and purchasers will need to take into account at a strategic level.

Self-test questions

Numbers in brackets refer to paragraphs where you can check your answers

1   How does Kotler define a market? (1.1)

2   Distinguish between a marketer's view of a market and an economist's view. (1.5)

3   List the four market structures in order of *increasing* competition. (1.8, Figure 3.1)

4   List the conditions for perfect competition. (2.1)

5   What is price discrimination? (3.4)

6   How might products in imperfectly competitive markets be differentiated? (4.2, 5.2)

7   What tactics are typically used by oligopoly suppliers? (5.2)

8   What are the advantages and disadvantages of dealing with (a) an oligopoly supplier and (b) an oligopoly customer? (5.12–5.14)

9   When do (a) buyers and (b) suppliers have more power in an industry? (6.6, 6.7)

10   List reasons why a firm might want to enter an international supply market. (7.6)

11   What are (a) the key drivers *for* and (b) the key arguments *against* globalisation? (7.13, 7.14)

CHAPTER 4

Demand and Supply

Assessment criteria and indicative content

2.2 Analyse the principles of market demand and supply and how these impact on procurement and supply

- Defining micro economics
- Demand and supply curves
- Shifts in demand and supply
- Elasticity of demand and supply

2.3 Explain the impact that market factors can have on organisations

- Market change
- The impact of demand and supply on pricing and availability
- The impact of product lifecycles on demand

Section headings

1. Micro economics
2. Demand and supply in practice
3. The product lifecycle

Introduction

The main focus of this chapter is concerned with how demand and supply for products and services are determined, and how the interaction of supply and demand determines the prices of products and services.

1   Micro economics

Defining micro economics

1.1 Micro economics is the study of how firms and individuals make decisions to allocate limited resources. In principle, there is no limit to the demand for goods and services: people and firms always want more. But there is a limit to their power of acquiring goods and services. This is because they must provide resources in exchange, and the available resources are always finite.

1.2 In studying micro economics we are looking at how firms behave in the markets they operate in: what goods they decide to produce, in what quantities, at what cost, and for what selling prices.

1.3 This is in contrast to macro economics, which is the study of overall economic activity, not the study of individuals and firms. Macro economics is concerned with 'big picture' issues such as economic growth or decline, inflation, unemployment and so on.

What is a market?

1.4 A market is a place where buyers and sellers of a product are brought together to trade. This may be a physical location where they interact face to face (like a supermarket or car showroom) – but it may equally well be 'cyber space' (as in online share trading, online stores and auction sites such as e-Bay) or a network of contacts with intermediaries (eg share brokers or export agencies) so that buyer and seller never deal directly with each other. In each case, the main features of a market are the exchange of goods or services and payment in some form.

1.5 **Product markets** are the markets in which a firm sells its products and services to consumers. **Supply (or factor) markets** are the markets in which a firm purchases the resources it needs for production (eg materials and labour). The purchasing function therefore deals primarily in various supply markets.

1.6 As we saw in an earlier chapter, a **market economy** (or **free market system**) is one in which basic economic choices (what to produce, how, for whom and at what price) are made through the market – by consumer choice – without state intervention. To understand how these choices are made you need to be familiar with a key economic concept: the market mechanism. This is the relationship between demand and supply for a particular product or service, and the way in which price affects both.

The market mechanism: demand and supply

1.7 *Demand* is the quantity of goods that consumers are willing and able to buy. It varies with price: in general, as the price of a good goes up, demand goes down – because some people will cut down on their purchases, or switch to cheaper substitutes.

1.8 However, this is a simplified picture, because other factors than price also impact on demand for products. We will return to this point later in the chapter.

1.9 It may help to see a very basic diagram of the relationship between price and demand, called a 'demand curve'. As prices rise, demand falls, as shown by a movement *along* the downward demand curve: Figure 4.1 (a). However, changes in the other determining factors lead to a *shift of the demand curve itself:* at *any* given price, demand may fall or rise: Figure 4.1 (b).

Figure 4.1 *Demand curve*

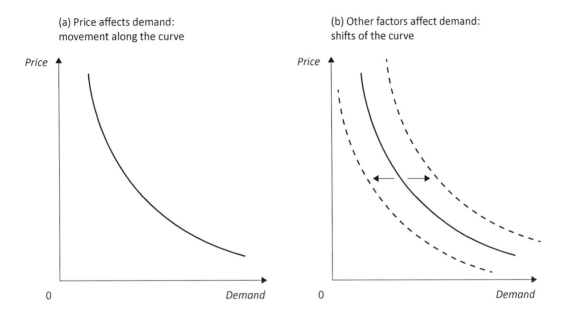

(a) Price affects demand:
movement along the curve

(b) Other factors affect demand:
shifts of the curve

1.10 *Supply* is the amount that firms are willing and able to sell. This too varies with price: in general, as the market price of a good rises, supply also rises – because higher prices mean greater profitability, increasing the willingness of firms to produce more.

1.11 Once again, other factors than price can affect supply and we will return to this point later.

1.12 Again, it may help to see a very basic diagram of the relationship between price and quantity of supply, called a 'supply curve'. As prices rise, supply also rises, as shown by a movement *along* the upward supply curve: Figure 4.2 (a). However, changes in the other determining factors lead to a *shift of the supply curve itself:* at *any* given market price, producers may raise or lower supply: Figure 4.2 (b).

Figure 4.2 *Supply curve*

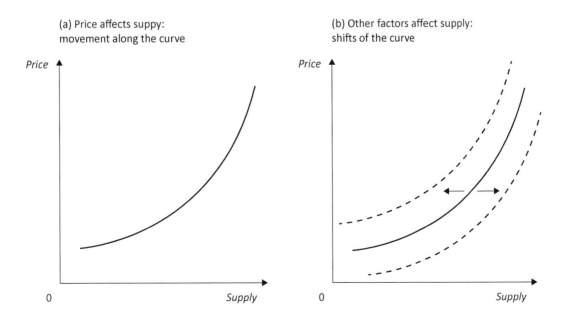

(a) Price affects suppy:
movement along the curve

(b) Other factors affect supply:
shifts of the curve

1.13 There is one price (called the **equilibrium price**) at which producers wish to sell the same amount as consumers wish to buy: in other words, the market 'clears' (without either surplus supply or unsatisfied demand).

1.14 Say that, at a certain price, supply exceeds demand. Goods will pile up in the shops – and the price will start to fall. Falling prices act as a signal to suppliers to cut back on supply – at the same time as increasing demand again. The market eventually stabilises at a price at which the supply of a good matches demand for that good: Figure 4.3. Both parties are relatively satisfied, so there is (for the moment) no need for further adjustment.

Figure 4.3 *Equilibrium price*

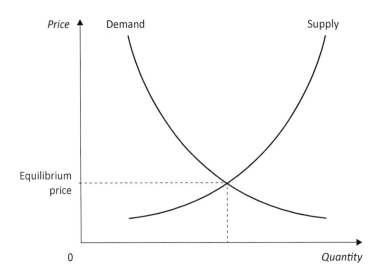

1.15 So by consuming a product at a given level at a given price, consumers are effectively determining the resources that will be devoted to production of that product: price is the economy's mechanism for allocating resources.

2 Demand and supply in practice

What determines the level of demand for a product?

2.1 Demand is the quantity of a good which consumers want, and are willing and able to pay for. If you think about how you decide which goods to buy, you will realise that there are many factors entering into the decision. The main influences on the demand for goods and services are discussed below.

2.2 **Price** is probably the most significant factor. The higher the price, the less likely people are to buy it. For a particular product, economists can create a **demand curve** – a graph indicating how demand falls as price rises. We saw an example of a demand curve earlier in the chapter.

2.3 In general, the more **income** people earn, the more they will buy. The demand for most goods increases as income rises.

2.4 Two or more goods are defined as **substitutes** if they are interchangeable (or almost interchangeable) in giving consumers utility. For example, margarine is a fairly close substitute for butter. If something has a substitute, you will probably compare the price of the substitute with the price of the good you are thinking of buying. Butter is more expensive than margarine, so, apart from the health considerations, you may decide to buy margarine. On the other hand, milk has very few substitutes, so your decision to buy it will not depend heavily on the price of other products.

2.5 Suppose the price of margarine rises. Even if it is still cheaper than butter, some people will decide that the difference in price is so small that they would rather buy butter. Demand for margarine will fall, while that for butter will rise.

2.6 Conversely, if the price of a substitute falls, then demand for the good in question will also fall, as people switch to the substitute.

2.7 If good A and good B are **substitutes**, a **rise** in the price of one will cause a **rise** in demand for the other, and *vice versa*.

2.8 **Complements** are goods which must be used together. For example, a compact disc player is no good without any compact discs. The price of a good's complements is very important when considering whether or not to buy it. You may be able to afford the player, but if you will not be able to buy any compact discs, there is little point in the purchase.

2.9 If the price of a **complement** rises, then demand for the good in question will **fall**. Conversely, if the price of a complement falls, demand for the good will rise.

2.10 **Taste** is influenced by many different things. You may decide not to buy butter purely on health grounds, having been made aware of its high cholesterol levels. Or fashion may induce you to buy a new pair of shoes even if you don't really need them and cannot afford them. Of all the factors influencing demand, taste is the most difficult one to quantify.

2.11 Clearly, the size of total demand depends on the number of people who are aware of the good's existence, who are able to obtain it and who are likely to want it. **Market size** can be altered by changes in the size and structures of the population. If the birth rate falls in an area, this will have a long-term effect on the total population size and will have a more immediate effect in reducing the number of babies, hence influencing the demand for prams, equipment and clothing designed for babies. It will, of course, also affect the demand for school places, for schoolteachers and for people to train teachers.

2.12 It is not only the volume and quality of **advertising** that can influence demand for a product but also the amount of advertising in comparison with that for competing products. Advertisers cannot often increase total consumption; more often they transfer it from one good to another.

2.13 A change in the **quality** of goods or services will have an effect on how much will be demanded at a particular price. An improvement in quality will increase demand.

What determines the level of supply of a product?

2.14 **Supply** is the quantity of a good which suppliers (or a single supplier) are willing and able to produce in a given period. As with demand, the decision about how much to supply depends on many factors, of which one of the most important is price. In the suppliers' case, the cost of production is also of paramount importance.

2.15 The higher the market **price** of the product, the more the supplier will wish to supply because he will make a bigger profit. For a particular product, economists can create a **supply curve** – a graph indicating how supply increases as price rises.

2.16 In producing goods for sale, the supplier will incur **costs**. Clearly, these must be covered if the supplier is to stay in business. The supplier will therefore compare the market price with his costs to make sure that production will be profitable. Costs will change over time, as technology and production methods change.

2.17 Certain industries are particularly susceptible to **uncontrollable factors**, such as changes in the weather. The most obvious example is agriculture, where bad weather can diminish or even obliterate supply. If the farmer is lucky he can smooth out some of the fluctuations by storing produce during good times and releasing his stocks during bad times, but not all goods can be stored.

2.18 **The level of technology** influences the efficiency with which capital or machines and labour can be used to produce goods. Improved technology enables firms to produce more with a given input of resources, ie at the same cost, and can thus be expected to increase the amount that they are willing to supply at given prices.

2.19 Advanced technology may not be worthwhile in some forms of production unless a certain minimum level of production is desired by customers. Firms may not, therefore, be willing to supply at all unless this level is reached. Alternatively, they may only be willing to supply at high prices because at low quantity levels they have to use expensive methods of production. There may then be two sets of supply conditions – one for low production levels at expensive production costs and one for high levels of production where advanced technology can be employed to reduce the production cost per unit.

2.20 **New entrants** to the supply market increase the supply of goods or services in that market.

2.21 The availability of **complements** is also important. Many goods are linked to each other – for example, cameras and films. A reduction in the price of cameras will mean that more cameras are supplied (at a lower price); this increase in demand will have a knock-on effect on the supply of films without any change in their price.

Shifts in demand and supply

2.22 Figure 4.1(a) shows how price and demand are related. As price rises, demand falls. If we plot this on the graph, we would indicate it by a movement from one point of the demand curve to another.

2.23 However, changes in other determinants of demand have the effect of shifting the entire demand curve to the left or right, as indicated by Figure 4.1(b). For example, suppose that the main curve in Figure 4.1(b) represents the demand for Product X. Now suppose that a new manufacturer enters the market with a rival product, Product Y, which is immediately perceived as very attractive. This has the effect of shifting the entire demand curve for Product X to the left, as indicated by the dotted line in Figure 4.1(b). What this means is that the level of demand for Product X is less than it used to be at all prices that the producer may charge.

2.24 There is a similar effect with supply curves. A change in price is plotted on the graph as a movement from one point of the supply curve to another: Figure 4.2(a). However, a change in any of the other determinants of supply is shown by a shift in the entire supply curve: Figure 4.2(b)

The interaction of supply and demand

2.25   Consumers want to pay as little as possible, but suppliers want to charge as much as possible. The two sides of the market have to compromise at some price between these two extremes. When the demand and supply curves are put together, **equilibrium price** is at the point of intersection and is the result of the interaction of demand and supply (refer back to Figure 4.3). It also ensures that demand and supply adjust until the quantities which consumers want to buy just equal the quantities which suppliers wish to sell, in a compromise which Adam Smith in his *Wealth of Nations* (1776) called 'the invisible hand'. In fact, there is a two-way relationship: price affects demand and supply; and demand and supply affect price.

Price elasticity of demand and supply

2.26   Price elasticity of demand is the degree of sensitivity of demand for a good to changes in the price of that good. Goods are described as 'inelastic' if the quantity of them demanded is relatively insensitive to the price charged. Typically such goods are basics, such as food, which people put at the top of their spending priorities. Conversely, demand is described as being 'elastic' where the quantity of a good demanded is relatively sensitive to a change in price. The phrase 'price elasticity of demand' is a bit long winded, so it is often shortened to 'elasticity of demand' or even PED.

2.27   Price elasticity is the proportionate change in demand divided by the proportionate change in the good's price. Although mathematically this can be defined in a number of ways, the most common formula is as follows.

$$PED = \frac{\text{Percentage change in quantity demanded}}{\text{Percentage change in price}}$$

Because an **increase** in price normally causes a **reduction** in the quantity demanded, the PED is normally negative. In fact this is so common that frequently the PED is stated without its minus sign, so beware!

2.28   As an example of this calculation, if PED for a certain good currently equals –2, how will sales be affected if price rises by 10 per cent? You should be able to see that there will be a fall of 20 per cent in the quantity demanded.

2.29   When PED > 1 (ie price elasticity of demand is greater than 1), demand is relatively elastic and the quantity demanded is very responsive to price changes; when PED < 1 (ie price elasticity of demand is less than 1), demand is relatively inelastic and the quantity demanded is not very responsive to price changes.

2.30   Note that if demand is said to be inelastic, this does not mean that there will be no change in quantity demanded when the price changes. It means that the consequent demand change will be **proportionately** smaller than the price change. If demand does not change at all after a price change, demand is said to be perfectly inelastic.

2.31   Price elasticity of demand will therefore be low for goods which are necessities or are habit forming because these have few substitutes in the perception of the consumer. Equally goods which have many substitutes and which represent a large proportion of consumer's expenditure have an elastic demand.

2.32 When demand is elastic, total revenue rises as price falls. This is because the quantity demanded is very responsive to price changes. A fall in the price gives rise to a **more** than proportionate rise in the quantity demanded. The net effect is that revenue (= price × quantity) rises.

2.33 Conversely, when demand is inelastic, total revenue falls as price falls. Here a fall in price causes a **less** than proportionate rise in quantity demanded, the result being a net fall in total revenue.

The relevance of elasticity to buyers

2.34 It is not an easy matter to estimate the elasticity of demand for a product. The judgement of expert analysts may be a helpful indicator. Customer surveys may also provide useful information. Some companies use field testing exercises to assess the effects of price changes on demand. In the last resort, though, it is not an exact science.

2.35 Despite this, buyers should not underestimate the usefulness of price elasticity. If a reasonable estimate can be formed of the elasticity of demand for a product, the information can be put to good use in a negotiation.

- If demand for a product is known to be inelastic, it may be unrealistic to hope for any price concessions from the supplier. The buyer should focus his negotiating effort on other areas.
- A buyer may be able to assess elasticity of demand for products of alternative suppliers. This can assist in making a choice between them.

2.36 Even if the supplier benefits from low price elasticity (enabling him to increase prices without losing business) it is not all bad news for the buyer. For one thing, the particular item may be only a small part of his total spend. For another, the buyer may be more interested in other factors, such as quality. Or the buying organisation may be so profitable that it can cope with price increases, and perhaps pass them on to its own customers.

3 The product lifecycle

3.1 The product lifecycle (PLC) is the concept that products pass through various stages in their sales life. In other words, demand for the product changes as the product matures and eventually (perhaps) declines. The PLC of products is depicted in Figure 4.4. The basic principle of the PLC is that products have a finite life. The length of the PLC will be different for all products. For example, the PLC of a chocolate bar will be very different from the PLC of a computer game.

3.2 You can see from Figure 4.4 that the PLC depicts the sales of a product over a period of time. An organisation should plot sales over a period of time and forecast or extrapolate future sales, based on this knowledge. This information is relatively easy to collect, especially with computer systems available which will manipulate sales information and produce the PLC for the marketer.

3.3 Conventionally, marketers distinguish five stages in the lifecycle: development, introduction, growth, maturity and decline. (Alternative analyses, perhaps involving four or six stages, are also possible.) Various characteristics can be associated with each of these stages.

Figure 4.4 *The product lifecycle*

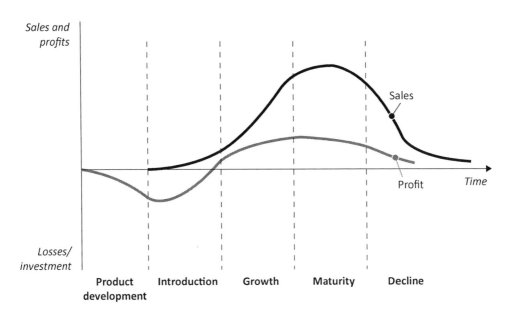

3.4 The **development stage** begins when the company finds and develops an idea for a new product. At this stage, the company is investing money without getting any return (because no sales are being made).

3.5 The **introduction stage** is when any product is launched into the market. Sales are low at this stage but a business will encourage sales to grow through promotions. Often, a company may be selling its products at a loss in the introduction stage of the PLC because of the cost of creating customer awareness and high research and development expenditure. However, there will be only a limited number of competitors at this stage if the product is innovative.

3.6 In the **growth stage** sales will increase and the business will be expecting to earn profit. The business will encourage repeat purchases for customers who bought the product in the introduction stage of the PLC. It will also encourage new users of the product. Profits will be evident and so it is at this stage of the PLC that a company must be ready for competition.

3.7 In the **maturity stage** sales continue to grow and eventually reach a level where they remain until the decline stage. Competition is at its height in the maturity stage and companies will compete to keep market share. A company will wish to extend the maturity stage of the PLC by finding new users for their products, increasing the frequency of use by current customers, reducing prices or changing packaging.

3.8 Before reaching the decline stage, products reach the **saturation stage** of the PLC. This is not indicated in Figure 4.4 because many authorities view the saturation phase as part of the maturity phase. During saturation, companies will face severe competition and reduced profits. Some companies will leave the market at this stage because prices are falling as a result of competition for market share. Additionally, the market is no longer growing.

3.9 Eventually, sales of almost any product will begin to fall because new or improved products have become available or the original product has been superseded by a newer model. The majority of businesses will aim to reduce costs at this **decline stage** of the PLC by spending less, or even nothing at all, on promotions. The objective now may be to get rid of any stocks of the product while there is at least some life left in the market and before demand dies. Businesses must be ready to launch new products onto the market to sustain revenue.

3.10   A partial explanation for the shape of the product lifecycle is to be found in the work of Everett Rogers. Rogers was interested in the readiness of individuals to adopt new products (the **diffusion of innovations**). He distinguished between five categories of individuals based on this criterion.

- **Innovators** are adventurous. They are quick to try new products, even though there is some risk (the products may prove to be unfashionable, or of poor quality).
- **Early adopters**, as the name suggests, are also relatively quick to try new products, but are not so adventurous as the first group. They are guided by respect, being opinion leaders in their community and adopting new ideas early but after careful consideration.
- The **early majority** are deliberate in their decisions. They are not leaders or opinion formers, but are still ready to adopt new products more quickly than the average.
- The **late majority** are sceptical. They wait for others to try new products. Only after a product has thoroughly proved itself will they commit to buying it.
- **Laggards** are cautious. They tend to distrust change and are slow to adopt new products. Being in favour of tradition, they tend to adopt only when the new product has itself become traditional.

3.11   Rogers's research enabled him to quantify these distinctions, as shown in Figure 4.5.

Figure 4.5 *Rogers's adopter categorisation*

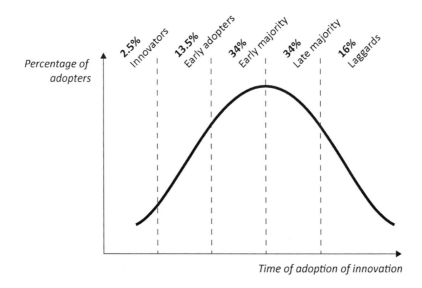

Using the PLC in product portfolio management

3.12   At introduction stage the product is basic and may not be of high quality. The reason for this may be associated with the high costs of launching the product. However, the producer will continually investigate the design of the product so that it can be more fully developed. Customer response to the product, and revenue generated by sales, both enable the company more easily to maintain competitive advantage by reinvesting in the product. It is at this time that the producer will consider new features and quality improvement, and therefore the product may be subject to frequent design changes.

3.13   By the growth stage of the PLC the quality of the product will have improved and the producer will have identified areas for product differentiation because of the number of competing products on the market. The producer may add new features to the product or improve the style of the basic product. The objective at this stage will be to sustain growth as long as possible and this may be at the expense of profit. However, the producer will hope for higher profits at the maturity stage through investment now.

3.14   During maturity, products become more standardised and differences between competing products are less distinct. Because of the number of competing products, the producer may concentrate on building the brand to encourage customer loyalty. The important issue at this stage is to extend the PLC so that sales of a product carry on for as long as possible.

3.15   Differentiation from competitors' products may be almost non-existent during decline. In fact, the producer may wish to rationalise the product and its features because he realises that resources should be allocated to other products in the growth and maturity stage of the PLC.

3.16   Overall, the producer will want to ensure that he is selling products which are at different stages in their lifecycle. An organisation which finds that most of its products are in decline must surely realise the difficulties it may face. Unless new products are introduced quickly, this organisation will not survive. However, this is not to say that it is not desirable to have some products at the decline stage of the PLC; after all, they are generating some revenue, even if it is limited.

3.17   On the other hand, a business does not want all its products at growth stage because it would be difficult to forecast with certainty how these products will perform in future and whether their lifecycle will be short or long.

Criticisms of the PLC

3.18   The PLC is a valuable planning tool but it does have some drawbacks which indicate that it is an aid which should not be used in isolation.

3.19   Drawbacks of the PLC include the following.

- The PLC can only be accurately plotted after sales have taken place. In the meantime, planning is based on forecasting and estimating.
- It is difficult to ascertain, except in hindsight, which stage of the cycle a product has reached. Remember that the PLC will never be completely smooth: there will be minor peaks and troughs which may be analysed incorrectly.
- The above problem may lead to misinterpretation and/or manipulation. For example, a marketing manager might decide to stop promoting the product because it has reached the decline stage. However, he might have misinterpreted a minor trough and, in effect, has encouraged the decline of that product's life. On the other hand, the marketing manager who has an emotional attachment to a product because of the time and effort he has invested, may wittingly or unwittingly interpret a minor peak during decline as a turning point.
- There is a temptation to decide, in advance, what the life of the product will be, therefore risking a shorter lifecycle by failing to take measures to extend it.
- The PLC curve is rarely smooth.
- The PLC does not provide specific direction for marketing strategy. It is an indicator only and will not provide definite answers.
- It assumes that all products follow a similar cycle.

Chapter summary

- A market is a 'place' where buyers and sellers interact. A market economy is one in which economic choices (what to produce, how, for whom, and at what price) are made by the market via the market mechanism: supply and demand.
- Demand (the amount of goods consumers want to buy) usually falls as prices rise, in a downward demand curve. Supply (the amount of goods firms want to produce) usually rises as prices rise, in an upward supply curve. The market eventually stabilises at a price where supply equals demand (equilibrium price).
- The demand for a product is determined by such factors as its price and quality, income levels, availability and price of substitutes and complements, customer tastes and advertising.
- The supply of a product is determined by such factors as its price, cost levels, random uncontrollable factors, level of technology, new entrants to the market, and availability and price of complements.
- The product lifecycle models the demand for a product over a period of time. It is usually analysed as comprising five stages: development; introduction; growth; maturity; and decline.

Self-test questions

Numbers in brackets refer to paragraphs where you can check your answers

1   Define micro economics. (1.1)

2   A typical demand curve slopes upwards from left to right. True or false? (Figure 4.1)

3   What is meant by the equilibrium price for a product? (1.13)

4   A rise in the price of a substitute causes a rise in the demand for the basic product. True or false? (2.7)

5   How can supply be affected by uncontrollable factors? (2.17)

6   Distinguish between a movement along a demand curve and a shift in the curve. (2.22, 2.23)

7   When demand is elastic, total revenue rises as price falls. True or false? (2.32)

8   List the five stages of the PLC. (Figure 4.4)

9   At what stage of a typical PLC will the producer start to earn profit? (3.6)

10 List the five categories of individuals identified by Everett Rogers in his analysis of product adoption. (3.10)

CHAPTER 5

The External Environment of Procurement

Assessment criteria and indicative content

 Use analytical tools to explain the impact of the external environment on procurement and supply

- The use of environmental scanning
- The use of PEST (political, economic, social and technological) criteria or STEEPLE (social, technological, economic, environmental, political, legislation and ethical) criteria that impacts on organisations' external environment

Section headings

1   What is the purchasing environment?
2   Why analyse the purchasing environment?
3   The STEEPLE framework
4   Other tools of analysis

Introduction

In this chapter, we start by defining the external environment of procurement, and explaining why it is an important area of study. We then go on to survey the main model used to categorise and analyse environmental factors (the STEEPLE model); sources of information for such an analysis; and ways in which an environmental analysis can be used by managers to make decisions for an organisation or purchasing function.

It is easy to get bogged down in technicalities and develop a compartmentalised view. However, it is important to retain an overview, and to get a sense for how the different aspects of the environment interrelate. This chapter should give you an integrated, introductory-level view. Later chapters will focus on specific areas in greater detail, and with more technical terminology.

1 What is the purchasing environment?

Micro and macro environments

1.1 The 'purchasing environment' is the 'macro' environment or context within which purchasing activity takes place.

1.2 The environment of a given purchasing function can be seen as a series of concentric circles: Figure 5.1.

- The internal environment of the organisation includes its various functions and personnel; its style or 'culture'; its objectives and plans; systems and technology; rules and procedures and so on.
- The immediate operating or micro environment of the organisation includes the customers, suppliers and competitors who directly impact on its operations.
- The general or macro environment incorporates wider factors in the market and society in which the organisation operates: industry structure, the national economy, law, politics, culture, technological development and natural resources.

Figure 5.1 *The purchasing environment*

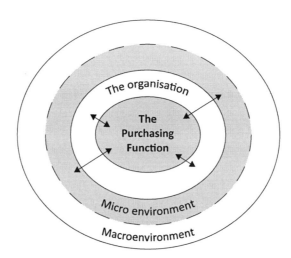

1.3 Purchasing activity will be strongly *influenced* by factors in all three 'tiers' of the environment: from internal purchasing procedures, to supplier changes, to national contract law or international commodity prices. In turn, a purchasing function has a measure of *influence* or control *over*:

- The *internal* environment (most obviously, by managing the flow of materials into and through the organisation) and
- The *micro* environment (most obviously, by seeking to manage supplier behaviour).

1.4 The 'macro' environment, however, is *not* generally within the organisation's control – however much it may seek to predict, manage or even influence events – and it is this part of the environment that is really referred to when we use the term 'purchasing environment'.

1.5 Throughout the remaining chapters of this Course Book we will explore a range of macro environmental factors and consider how they influence purchasing decisions.

Local, national and international environments

1.6 As well as distinguishing between 'micro' and 'macro' environments, it is possible to classify environmental factors according to their *scale:* that is, whether they affect a local, national, international or global sphere. Here are some examples.

- Local factors might include local authority byelaws and planning regulations that affect the activities of an organisation within its local area.
- National factors might include the business law and government policy affecting a company within the UK (or other country of operation).
- International factors (affecting more than one nation) might include exchange rates for the currencies of two or more nations, which affect trading between those nations, and the formation of trading blocs such as the European Union (EU).
- Global factors (affecting all nations) might include industrialisation, technological development or global warming.

1.7 A given purchasing organisation will be subject to the law, regulation, social customs and technological limitations of the country in which it operates: its national environment. However, it is increasingly likely also to be subject to the same kinds of factors as they apply in *other* countries, or *across* national boundaries. This will certainly be the case in any of the following situations.

- The organisation has subsidiaries, or works with customers or suppliers, in other countries.
- Its country of operation is part of an international political or economic 'bloc' (such as the EU), where international laws, trading agreements and shared social policies apply to all members.
- Its activities are subject to genuinely international or global influences, such as international law, global commodity prices or climate change.

1.8 **Globalisation** itself is one of the major current trends in the purchasing environment. It has been driven by factors such as the following.

- Improvements in transport technology, creating the 'shrinking' of distance for the physical movement of goods
- Improvements in information and communication technology or ICT (including the e-commerce potential of the internet), abolishing distance for the purposes of communication
- Reduction in the financial and administrative barriers to imports and exports (eg through the formation of trading blocs and agreements such as the European Economic Area)
- Convergence in cultural values and consumer tastes (due to increased travel and global media), creating markets for global brands such as Coca-Cola or McDonald's
- The business benefits of international trade: access to larger markets, economies of scale, the ability to outsource activities to low-cost-labour economies and so on.

1.9 In this Course Book, much of our detailed discussion will necessarily focus on the UK or EU environment, but we will remind you of the international context where relevant to the syllabus.

The stakeholder environment

1.10 Stakeholders are individuals and groups who have an interest or 'stake' in an organisation, project or activity – whether because they are participants or investors in it, or because it affects them significantly in some way. Key stakeholders in purchasing activity, for example, may include:

purchasing staff; senior management; other functions relying on the timely supply of materials; the organisation's suppliers and potential suppliers; customers relying on product quality and timely delivery; regulatory and industry bodies; and, arguably, the wider community which benefits from ethical and sustainable purchasing.

1.11 Stakeholders form an important part of the purchasing environment.

- They may seek to influence the organisation, if they perceive that their interests are threatened. Some stakeholder groups will have more power than others. Staff and/or suppliers may negotiate for better terms, for example, or activists may threaten a boycott if the organisation uses environmentally-unsound or labour-exploiting suppliers.
- There is strong public and regulatory pressure for business organisations to be 'socially responsible': taking into account the wider social and environmental impacts of their activities on a range of stakeholders.
- Organisations themselves increasingly follow (and publicise) ethical frameworks, acknowledging their responsibility not to trample on stakeholders' interests – whether or not they have an influential 'voice' in the matter.

1.12 Since stakeholders can be within the organisation or purchasing department, within its immediate trading networks and/or in its wider field of operations, the 'stakeholder environment' effectively cuts through the boundaries between the internal, micro and macro environments: Figure 5.2.

Figure 5.2 *The stakeholder environment*

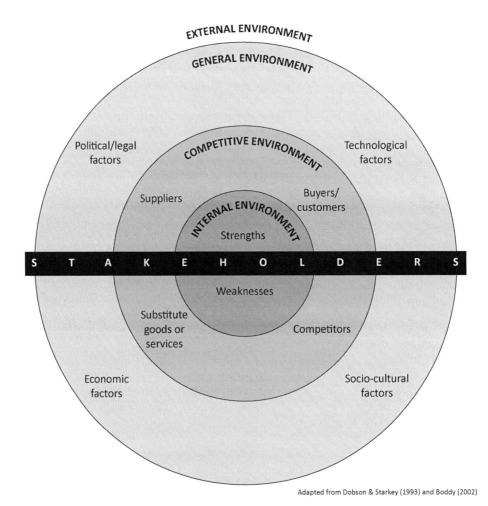

Adapted from Dobson & Starkey (1993) and Boddy (2002)

2 Why analyse the purchasing environment?

The organisation as an open system

2.1 If you're going to study this topic effectively, it helps to know why it's important – and how the knowledge and tools you acquire will help you in a purchasing job. Why do purchasing managers analyse the purchasing environment, and monitor changes to it over time, and take it into account in making their decisions? The answer lies partly in the definition of a **system.**

2.2 A system is 'an entity which consists of interdependent parts'.

- A **closed system** is one which operates entirely separately from its environment, needing nothing from it and contributing nothing to it.
- An **open system** is a system which is connected to, and interacts with, its environment. It receives various 'inputs' from its environment and converts these into 'outputs' to the environment. Feedback information (Did we get the result we wanted? Does something need to be changed?) enables the system to change its behaviour in order to stay stable in a changing environment.

2.3 An organisation can be seen as an open system: Figure 5.3

Figure 5.3 *The organisation as an open system*

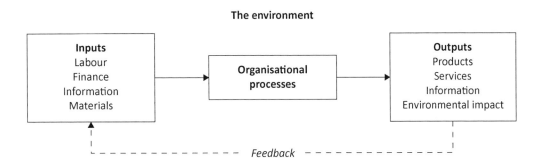

2.4 The open systems model emphasises the importance of taking the environment into account. Firstly, because an organisation *depends* on its environment as the source of its inputs; the market for its outputs; and a key source of feedback information to measure and adjust its performance. And secondly, because an organisation also *impacts* on its environment, in the process of taking in inputs and creating outputs (both products, such as goods and services, and 'by products' such as waste, pollution or local employment).

2.5 The purchasing function is particularly important in this context, because buyers – by means of their contacts with the external supply market – span the boundary between the organisation and its environment (as shown in Figure 5.1). The marketing function performs a similar role by means of its contacts with external customers.

2.6 The environment will therefore exert a strong influence on an organisation's strategy, activity and performance, in various ways.

- It presents *threats* (such as restrictive legislation, competitor initiatives, technology obsolescence or industrial action by trade unions, say) and *opportunities* (such as growth in market demand, technological improvements or more skilled workers entering the labour pool). These affect the organisation's ability to compete in its market and fulfil its objectives.

Environmental threats and opportunities are key factors in the formation of business strategies and plans.

- It is the source of *resources* needed by the organisation (labour, materials and supplies, plant and machinery, energy, finance, information and so on). Environmental factors determine to what extent these resources are, or are not, available in the right quantity, at the right time and at the right price.
- It contains *stakeholders* who may seek, or have the right, to influence the activities of the organisation. An organisation must comply with laws and regulations, for example, in order to avoid legal and financial penalties, but it may also have to negotiate with employees, suppliers and customers – or bow to public opinion which might jeopardise its market or reputation.

2.7 So purchasing officers, among other managers, must analyse and understand the environmental factors affecting their organisation. But that's only the beginning – because those factors are also constantly *changing*.

Environmental change

2.8 Change in the environment often creates a need (or opportunity) for change in an organisation's plans and activities. A purchasing function, for example, may need to respond to any or all of the following factors.

- Emerging economic opportunities and threats, such as the opening up of new supply markets, falling or rising prices for critical supplies, or competitors tying up the best sources of supply
- Changes in social values, preferences and expectations, which may give rise to demand for new or modified products (eg recyclable materials) or business processes (eg purchasing over the internet) or higher expectations on the part of suppliers and other stakeholders (eg for 'fair trade' dealings)
- Environmental ('green') considerations, including the increasing scarcity of resources – and changes in consumer perceptions. A purchasing function may have to develop plans for sustainable sourcing, eco-friendly materials, pollution and waste management, for example.
- Technological developments: supporting new products and business methods, while rendering others obsolete
- The move from a national to an international and ultimately (perhaps) to a global economy, changing corporate structures, communication systems and supply chain strategies
- Constant amendments and additions to the law and regulation of business activities by the EU, national governments and other agencies.

The nature of environmental change

2.9 The precise nature, direction and pace of environmental change will depend on the organisation, its industry and its market. What major changes or trends can you see impacting major supermarkets, say, or local grocery stores? What about banks, travel and tourism operators, or car manufacturers? What about your own work organisation?

2.10 What we can say is that most business environments are getting both more *complex* (more interrelated factors to take into account) and more *dynamic* (faster and more wide-reaching change) – forcing organisations to adapt.

2.11 Strategy gurus Johnson & Scholes *(Exploring Corporate Strategy)* argue that the main problem posed for organisations by their environments is uncertainty, arising from complexity and dynamism.

- In a complex environment, there are a variety of influences which may impact on the organisation. These may be interrelated, so that change in one factor causes change in another. A high degree of knowledge is needed to cope with the environment.
- In a dynamic environment, change is driven by significant and powerful forces. A dynamic economy, for example, is one which is growing rapidly due to forces such as expanding global demand, the increased use of information technology or deregulation.

2.12 Organisations will need to assess the degree of uncertainty in their environments, and identify trends or directions of change, in order to measure and manage risk. Businesses often use historical data (what has happened in the past) in order to plan for the future (by building on past experience, or extrapolating past trends into the future). This is effective in stable or slow-changing environments – but dynamic or fast-changing environments require a more discontinuous, future-oriented perspective: What is likely to happen? What *might* happen? What threats and opportunities may emerge? How might things be different in five or ten years time?

2.13 Complex and dynamic environments require a new set of core competencies from organisations: the ability to be flexible or adaptable, and to respond swiftly (and without trauma) to constant and perhaps unforeseeable change.

- Organisations may need to adapt their processes and structures so that they can change direction swiftly if they need to. This may mean using versatile (multi-skilled) or cross-functional teams, which can be flexibly allocated to different tasks. It may mean improving communication in the organisation, so that environmental information (including shifts in customer demand) flows swiftly up to the top-level decision makers – and so that response plans and decisions flow swiftly back down for implementation.
- Organisations may need to develop strategies on a short time-horizon, rather than planning 5 or 10 years ahead, in order to stay sensitive and responsive to changing needs. Environmental scanning will become an important part of strategic management, ensuring that the organisation is aware of emerging threats and opportunities. Organisational strategy and change may be implemented in small steps or increments, allowing for review and adjustment at each stage.
- Organisations may need to improve their risk analysis and contingency planning, in order to minimise the risks of uncertainty, and to be prepared (as far as possible) for unpredictable changes.

2.14 Another term you might hear in relation to environmental change is 'turbulence'. Turbulence is the degree of volatility or instability in an environment, making it liable to sudden, unpredictable and potentially massive changes. Turbulence may arise from factors such as: changing governments or political instability, civil unrest or warfare; panic on the financial markets at the threat of recession, arising from the US mortgage lending crisis; the collapse of the value of particular currencies; or changes in a regional balance of power due to the economic growth of particular nations (eg the emergence of Pacific Rim manufacturing).

2.15 In addition, you should be aware of the potential for single unpredictable or 'catastrophic' events to disrupt business (and supply chains). What was the effect of the SARS virus outbreak on the travel industry, for example, and how could organisations such as airlines respond? What risks might be faced by buyers with key suppliers in areas prone to earthquakes or tsunamis? How might they make contingency plans for the risks, or respond to the risk event if it happens? What would be the effect on different types of businesses of the collapse of share prices and investor and consumer confidence as a result of the global financial crisis?

2.16   Get used to asking such questions of just about any headline you see in the quality press. What's going on here? What effect might this have on organisations of different types? How might this affect their supply chains, or disrupt supply, or raise (or lower) the price of materials?

Environmental analysis

2.17   Johnson & Scholes suggest that in order for an organisation to interact effectively with its environment, it must first analyse it systematically. An adapted version of their framework for environmental analysis is shown in Figure 5.4.

Figure 5.4   *Steps in environmental analysis*

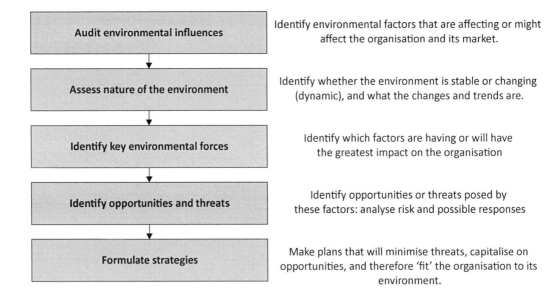

Audit environmental influences	Identify environmental factors that are affecting or might affect the organisation and its market.
Assess nature of the environment	Identify whether the environment is stable or changing (dynamic), and what the changes and trends are.
Identify key environmental forces	Identify which factors are having or will have the greatest impact on the organisation
Identify opportunities and threats	Identify opportunities or threats posed by these factors: analyse risk and possible responses
Formulate strategies	Make plans that will minimise threats, capitalise on opportunities, and therefore 'fit' the organisation to its environment.

2.18   In the following sections of this chapter we will look briefly at some of the tools used in this process.

Environmental scanning

2.19   As well as environmental analysis for formal strategic planning, most large organisations would carry out some form of environmental scanning. This involves continually gathering and analysing intelligence from sources such as professional, industry and trade journals and their websites; conferences and exhibitions; published reports and online databases (such as Mintel); published statistical sources such as *Social Trends* and the *Economic & Labour Market Review*; and so on.

2.20   The organisation may also retain specialist consultants or advisers who have knowledge, experience and contacts relevant to a particular aspect of the environment – such as technology, law or social trends – or who specialise in the discipline of environmental analysis and risk management.

2.21   However, one of the key roles of *any* manager (as identified by Henry Mintzberg) is that of 'Monitor': scanning the environment for information about changes, trends, threats and opportunities. This is one of the reasons for networking within your profession (other people are a great source of information), as well as reading quality newspapers and professional journals, and searching the internet with your eyes open.

2.22 In this Course Book we will highlight and explain the key environmental factors and trends commonly monitored by organisations – which should be a sufficient basis for exam answers. Given the nature of this paper, we strongly recommend that you browse through *Supply Management* and quality newspapers (and their online versions), and start a file of notes or cuttings on environmental issues and changes affecting purchasing in different types of organisations – including your own. (Examiners always appreciate the illustration of theory with real-life examples.)

2.23 We will now get an overview of some of the main tools used to analyse the purchasing environment in its various aspects.

3 The STEEPLE framework

Acronyms for environmental analysis

3.1 A popular tool for analysing the macro environment is described by the acronym PEST (and more comprehensive variants), which sets out the main categories of environmental factors which impact on organisations.

3.2 It is well worth remembering these categories. You can use whichever version is most readily applicable.

Political/legal	Socio-cultural	Political	Socio-cultural
Economic	Legal	Economic	Technological
Socio-cultural	Economic	Socio-cultural	Economic
Technological	Political	Technological	Environmental
	Technological	Legal	Political
		Environmental	Legal
			Ethical

Political factors

3.3 The political environment embraces factors such as: the policies of national governments and wider political bodies such as the EU; State support for industry (eg regional grants or industry subsidies, or assistance to small firms); the strength or weakness of trade unions; the influence of lobbying groups and public opinion on government policy; and the stability of governing regimes and other forms of political risk (particularly in international markets).

3.4 Sources of political information include: published government policy; direct contact with government or trade union representatives and lobbyists; media analysis of the political scene; published, online or specially commissioned surveys and reports; and specialist consultancies dealing in political risk analysis.

Economic factors

3.5 The macro-economic environment embraces the general level of activity and growth in the economic system, and the effect of economic 'boom and bust' cycles. This is related to more detailed economic factors such as a government's fiscal (tax) and monetary (money supply) policy; interest and foreign exchange rates; inflation; consumer spending; labour costs and unemployment levels; international trade agreements and so on.

3.6 Making informed judgements and assumptions about future macro-economic events is crucially important for planning business strategy. Think about the effects on purchasing of import taxes or exchange rate fluctuations, raising the cost of supplies; or rising UK labour costs, making it more attractive to source labour-intensive supplies from low-labour-cost countries; or quota limits on imports, restricting supply. (In a recent example, the EU imposed quotas on clothing imports from China – leaving UK retailers short of stock to meet demand, and scrambling to find alternative sources of supply.)

3.7 Organisations also operate within the more immediate economic environment of a business sector, industry and market. We have looked at some of these micro economic factors in earlier chapters.

3.8 Sources of economic data include: published government forecasts, reports and statistics; media analysis; industry projections and reports; and industry conferences and contacts.

Socio-cultural factors

3.9 The socio-cultural environment embraces 'people' aspects of the society in which the organisation operates and from which it draws its suppliers, customers and workers. Socio-cultural factors include: demographic characteristics (age, gender and geographical distribution, population density and movements, educational and occupational trends); cultural norms, values and customs; lifestyle and fashion trends; and so on. These factors reflect the needs and expectations of the organisation's target market and customers, and will obviously be taken into account when developing marketing plans. However, they also reflect other stakeholder groups: shaping relationships with suppliers from different cultures, say, and affecting the availability of the skilled labour needed by the organisation.

3.10 Sources of socio-cultural data include: published demographic surveys and reports (eg the *Economic and Labour Market Review*); media and specialist analysis of trends; market research programmes and consultancies and/or access to their published research reports; stakeholder feedback (eg customer, supplier or employee surveys); and general 'scanning' of the environment.

Technological factors

3.11 The technological environment embraces the technological sophistication of the organisation's national or international markets, and developments in the particular fields that are relevant to the organisation. Technology becomes more important every day, as innovations and developments have the following effects.

- Increasing the speed and power of information gathering, processing and communication (via information and communications technology or ICT) – supporting streamlined, automated, 'paperless' purchasing processes, for example

- Enabling 24/7 global business activity, via the World Wide Web – supporting international and global purchasing
- Enabling new products (such as music downloads and digital cameras) and new business processes (such as e-commerce and computer-assisted design and manufacture) – to which purchasing must adapt
- Shortening the shelf life of products (or 'product lifecycles'), due to the increasing pace of modification and obsolescence – creating pressure for product innovation, with fast, flexible supply chains to support it
- Changing industry structures and activities. (Think about the impact of digital cameras on photographic services, for example, or the impact of the internet on entertainment and travel booking agencies – and the implications for purchasing in both industries.)
- Creating 'virtual' teams and organisations, in which people share data and work together linked mainly by ICT, regardless of their physical location.

3.12 Information on the technology environment is available from: technology surveys; specialist journals; media analysis; trade conferences and exhibitions; technology-based consultancies and providers (eg R&D companies, software and systems developers, robotics companies and so on).

Environmental factors

3.13 The natural environment embraces factors such as: legislation, international obligations (such as the Kyoto agreement on climate change) and government targets in regard to environmental protection and sustainability; consumer and pressure-group demand for eco-friendly products and business processes; issues of pollution, waste management, disposal and recycling; the depletion of non-renewable natural resources; the protection of habitats and biodiversity from urbanisation and industry; the reduction of carbon emissions; the risk of natural forces (such as weather) affecting supply; and so on.

3.14 All these factors will impact on purchasing activity in areas such as materials specification; supplier selection and management (to ensure good environmental practice); logistics (eg transport) and reverse logistics (eg returns and recycling) planning; and compliance and risk management. Specific industries and firms will also have particular concerns: you might like to think what 'green' issues might be a priority for a car manufacturer, an airline, a brand of canned tuna or a hospital, say; or what kinds of supply are most likely to be subject to weather risk.

Legal factors

3.15 The legal environment includes the operation of the justice system (the law and how it is enforced) and the organisation's contractual relationships with various parties (including suppliers, customers and employees). There is a wide range of national and trans-national (eg EU) law and regulation on issues such as: commercial contracts; the rights of employers and employees; health and safety at work; consumer protection; environmental protection; data protection; public sector procurement; and so on. In addition to principles laid down by statute, there are principles developed by judges' decisions in the courts, which determine how the law is interpreted. Compliance with relevant legal provisions is essential both to demonstrate ethical behaviour (an important objective for many organisations) – and to avoid penalties and sanctions for *not* doing so.

3.16 Information on legal provisions and changes is well-publicised, and regularly scrutinised by specialist advisers. However, purchasing professionals will need to keep up to date with developments in their own areas of interest: *Supply Management*, for example, offers regular briefings and updates on relevant law and cases.

Ethical factors

3.17 The ethical environment, if you choose to add it to the mix, embraces a range of issues to do with corporate social responsibility and business ethics: what constitutes 'right conduct' for an organisation in its context. This overlaps with the legal and ecological environments, since compliance and environmental protection are generally regarded as ethical responsibilities. However, it also includes industry and professional Codes of Practice and stakeholder pressure in areas such as: fair trading and the ethical treatment of suppliers; the fair and humane treatment of employees (over and above legal minimum requirements); supporting local communities (with investment and employment); and selecting and managing suppliers so that *they* comply with good practice in these areas.

3.18 Industry associations and professional bodies such as CIPS often publish Codes of Ethics to provide guidelines in these areas. Many organisations also develop their own objectives for corporate citizenship or corporate social responsibility, and codes of ethics or codes of practice to support them. Debate in the media, attitude and feedback surveys, and the activities of pressure groups are also good sources of information about the ethical concerns of the wider stakeholder environment.

Using a PESTLE analysis

3.19 Having gathered and classified information on critical factors, changes and trends, using the PESTLE framework, managers can consider the implications for their organisation. A broad example of the kind of analysis that can be conducted, to support planning and decision-making, is shown in Table 5.1. Obviously, more specific factors or changes would raise more specific questions.

Table 5.1 *PESTLE analysis*

FACTOR	DESCRIPTION	ANALYSIS
Political	Government influence on your industry	What are the likely implications of a change in government policy?
Economic	Growth trends; patterns of employment, income, interest, exchange, tax rates etc.	How might changes affect future demand for your products and services, or future supply and cost of resources/labour?
Socio-cultural	Changing composition, attitudes, values, consumption patterns and education of the population	How might changes affect the demands and expectations of customers, suppliers and other stakeholders, or skill availability?
Techno-logical	Changing tools for design and manufacturing, information and communications etc.	Are there opportunities for development – or risks of obsolescence? Are competitors adapting more quickly?
Legal	Law and regulation on business, employment, information etc.	How will the organisation need to adapt its policies and practices in order to comply with forthcoming measures?
Ecological	Resources, sustainability, pollution and impact management, weather, 'green' pressures	Which factors may cause supply or logistical problems, compliance issues, market pressure or risk to reputation?

4 Other tools of analysis

4.1 Having audited the environment and gathered information on factors which might affect its activities and plans, the organisation needs to take action accordingly.

- Prioritise factors for problem-solving: that is, identify which are likely to have the greatest impact
- Identify whether and to what extent the factors represent opportunities or threats, to which the organisation must respond in order to stay competitive.

Two simple tools can be used for these purposes: the impact assessment grid and SWOT analysis. (Your syllabus also specifies the Five Forces Model, but we have already discussed this in Chapter 3: refer back if you need to refresh your memory.)

Impact assessment

4.2 Various CIPS Chief Assessors have highlighted this technique for evaluating environmental information, so although it is not specifically mentioned in the syllabus, it is worth looking at briefly. An impact (or risk) assessment grid is a two-by-two grid on which factors, changes or events can be plotted according to (a) the likelihood of their happening and (b) the seriousness of their effect if they do happen: Figure 5.5.

Figure 5.5 *Impact assessment grid*

		Impact/effect on organisation	
		Low	High
Likelihood of occurrence	Low	A	C
	High	B	D

4.3 Taking the segments of the grid one by one:

- Segment A will contain events which are not likely to happen and would have little effect if they did: say, a power failure at all suppliers' factories at once, when they all have emergency back-up generators. Given the low level of impact, the organisation can safely *ignore* such factors as low-priority.
- Segment B will contain events which are relatively likely to occur, but will not have a major effect: say, an exchange rate fluctuation, if the organisation is not heavily exposed in this area. The appropriate response is to *monitor* such factors, in case the situation changes and the impact may be greater than expected.
- Segment C will contain events which are not likely to happen, but will have a big impact if they do: say, the sinking of a ship with a cargo of critical supplies. The appropriate response is to draw up a *contingency plan* to minimise the impact, in case the event occurs: perhaps having a back-up source of supply, and insurance.
- Segment D will contain events which are both likely to happen and serious in their impact: say, a major new tax on your product, or the discovery of a new technology that will alter products and processes in an industry. The appropriate response is to *respond* to the perceived threat or opportunity, including it in strategic analysis and planning.

SWOT analysis

4.4 Strengths, Weaknesses, Opportunities and Threats analysis is a strategic planning technique, used to assess the internal resources of the organisation (or a function such as purchasing) to cope with and/or capitalise on factors in its environment.

4.5 Strengths and weaknesses are *internal* aspects of the business that enhance or limit its ability to compete, change and thrive. Internal appraisal may cover aspects such as the following.

- Physical and financial resources: plant and machinery, availability of raw materials, owned assets, revenue-earning potential, profitability
- The product and service portfolio, and its competitive strength (eg brand positioning and market share)
- Human resources: management expertise, staff skills, labour flexibility
- The efficiency and effectiveness of functions and operations (eg production, marketing, purchasing and supply)
- The efficiency and effectiveness of systems (eg for quality control, inventory management, communication, information processing)
- Organisation structure: adaptability, efficiency, co-ordination, teamwork
- Distinctive competencies: things the organisation does better than its competitors.

4.6 Opportunities and threats are factors in the *external environment* that may emerge to impact on the business. What potential do they offer to either enhance or erode competitive advantage or profitability?

4.7 Internal and external factors can be mapped in a SWOT grid as follows: Figure 5.6.

Figure 5.6 *SWOT analysis*

INTERNAL	**Strengths** New technology Quality management systems Stable, high quality staff Market leading brands	**Weaknesses** Low new product development Poor financial controls Non-renewable resources
EXTERNAL	**Opportunities** E-commerce Consumer values re quality Tax breaks for regional development	**Threats** Environmental protection law Fashion trends Ageing demographic

4.8 SWOT is used to identify areas where strategic responses are required in order for the organisation to maintain or enhance its position in relation to the environment.

- Plan to build on strengths and/or minimise weaknesses – in order to be able to capitalise on the identified opportunities (or create new ones) and to cope better with the identified threats.
- Plan to convert threats into opportunities – by developing the strengths (and contingency plans) to counter them more effectively than competitors, and by being prepared to learn from them.

Chapter summary

- The purchasing environment is the macro or wider environment or context within which purchasing takes place. It includes external factors which are largely outside the organisation's direct control. These may be local, national, international or global.
- Stakeholders are individuals and groups who have a legitimate interest or stake in the organisation's activities. They are a feature of the internal, micro and macro environments of the organisation, and an important influence on its policies.
- The organisation can be seen as an open system, connected to and interacting with its environment: taking in inputs and influences from the environment and creating outputs to the environment. The environment will therefore exert a strong influence on organisation strategy and activity, as a source of market threats and opportunities, resources and stakeholder influence.
- Environmental factors are subject to constant change, so organisations must monitor their environments in order to respond effectively (and if possible, proactively) to changing opportunities and threats.
- The PESTLE framework is used to categorise macro environment factors as: Political, Economic, Socio-cultural, Technological, Legal and Environmental. (An extra 'E' for Ethical factors may also be added: STEEPLE.)
- Other tools of analysis include: impact/risk assessment (to prioritise environmental factors affecting the organisation); Strengths, Weaknesses, Opportunities, Threats analysis (to identify threats that need to be neutralised and opportunities that can be capitalised on); and financial analysis (to analyse the financial strength and stability of the organisation and its suppliers and competitors).

Self-test questions

Numbers in brackets refer to paragraphs where you can check your answers

1   Distinguish between the micro and macro environments. (1.2–1.4)

2   List three factors driving globalisation. (1.8)

3   Why are stakeholders important in the purchasing environment? (1.11)

4   Describe an open system, and suggest its relevance to the study of the purchasing environment. (2.4, 2.5)

5   Give three examples of environmental change affecting purchasing. (2.8)

6   How can a purchasing manager contribute to environmental scanning? (2.19–2.21)

7   What does 'STEEPLE' stand for? (3.2)

8   Give two examples of each of the STEEPLE factors. (3.3, 3.5, 3.9, 3.11, 3.13, 3.15, 3.17)

9   Explain each of the segments in (a) an impact assessment grid, and (b) a SWOT analysis grid. (4.3, 4.5–4.7)

CHAPTER 6

Economic Factors

Assessment criteria and indicative content

3.2 Explain the implications of economic criteria that impact on procurement and supply

- Macro economic criteria such as interest rates, inflation, exchange rates, level of economic activity (GDP/GNP) that impact on organisations
- Micro economic criteria such as demand and supply that impact on organisations

Section headings

1. The economic environment
2. The national economy
3. The business cycle
4. International economics
5. Exchange rates
6. The economics of international sourcing

Introduction

In this chapter, we begin our detailed survey of the STEEPLE factors which make up the wider macro environment of organisations.

The term 'macro-economics' refers to the study of a whole economy – while 'micro-economics' refers to the study of economics as it applies to individual markets, products and firms (such as market supply and demand and market structures, which we discussed in Chapter 4). In this chapter, we look at some of the key macro-economic factors in the purchasing environment.

We start by giving you an overview of how national economies are managed, and how macro-economic factors impact on purchasing.

We go on to look at key concepts and factors in the national economy, including economic activity and growth, and the effects of unemployment, inflation and interest rates. We then show how many of these factors come together in the business cycle of 'booms and busts' (which may be familiar to you from headlines about 'downturn' and 'recession' during the global financial crisis).

In the final three sections of the chapter, we turn our attention to international economics, examining concepts such as the balance of payments, the impact of exchange rates on firms dealing in international markets, and the economic arguments for and against international sourcing.

1 The economic environment

National economic policy

1.1 It is the role of government to manage or control a national economy, in order to provide a stable economic framework from which, ideally, sustainable growth can be achieved.

1.2 The objective of a government's economic policies may be: to achieve sustainable growth in the economy; to control inflation; to achieve low unemployment levels; or to achieve a balance between exports and imports. (It is worth noting that the emphasis on these objectives changes in line with political, social and economic events.)

1.3 In order to achieve these objectives, a government will use a number of different policy tools. For example, *monetary policy* is the government's decisions and actions regarding the level of interest rates and the supply of money in the economy; while *fiscal policy* is the government's decisions and actions regarding the balance between taxation revenue and public expenditure.

Impact on purchasing

1.4 Macro-economic factors affect purchasing in a number of ways.

- The amount of economic activity determines the wealth of a nation, which influences the amount of disposable income its citizens have to spend – which in turn influences the demand for goods and services of various kinds, and the prices at which they can be sold. Lower demand and prices will affect the volume of procurement, and the budget available: on the other hand, it may enhance the role of purchasing, by focusing on the need for cost savings.
- Economic variables determine the strength of an economy and the extent of business confidence in it, which in turn influences the amount people are willing to invest. Changes in the level of investment spending (by both the private and public sectors) are major causes of the upswings and downswings in economic activity which we call business cycles – which again affect demand and prices.
- Employment and unemployment levels may affect the availability of labour and labour costs, as well as disposable incomes and demand.
- Rates of inflation affect prices, and therefore supply costs. They may also make imports relatively expensive or inexpensive, altering a firm's sourcing strategy.
- The overall rate of taxation affects the level of demand in an economy (eg less tax means more disposable income for consumers to spend), and the taxation of specific products (such as alcohol and tobacco) may impact on specialised businesses. At the same time, tax incentives and penalties may influence firms' operational policies (eg 'polluter pays' taxes).
- Exchange rate fluctuations create risk in international sourcing, potentially making foreign currency purchases (imports) more expensive.
- Interest rate fluctuations create risk for corporate finance, potentially making loans more expensive: this will have an impact on companies borrowing to purchase large capital items, for example.

1.5 Basically, any factor that increases *demand* for an organisation's product will also increase its need for *inputs*. Any factor that decreases demand will reduce the need for inputs – but will place more importance on the potential for the purchasing function to control or reduce the costs of those inputs.

1.6 We will now look more closely at some of the key concepts.

2 The national economy

Economic activity

2.1 An economy is a system, which – like the organisation system we looked at in Figure 5.3 – takes in inputs and converts them into outputs. Economic activity can be portrayed as a 'flow' of economic resources into organisations which produce outputs for consumers, which then generates a return flow of income through consumer expenditure.

2.2 One way of portraying this flow of resources and income between firms and domestic households, is as follows: Figure 6.1.

Figure 6.1 *The flow of economic resources*

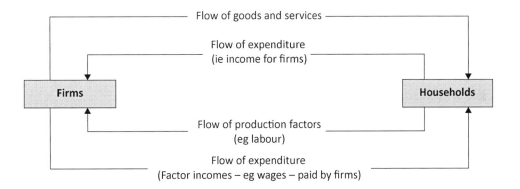

2.3 Total spending in a given economy, however, consists not just of consumer (domestic household) spending, but also of government spending (on providing public services), investment spending (by other firms, on capital items such as plant and machinery) and export spending (foreign purchasers buying our goods). In addition, some household resources are taken out of the flow in the form of tax, savings and import spending (buying foreign goods). The picture is therefore more as follows: Figure 6.2

Figure 6.2 *The circular flow of national income*

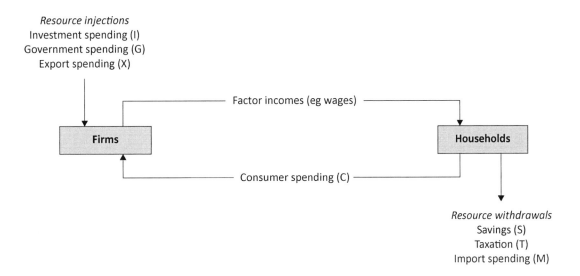

2.4 Total spending – or 'aggregate demand' – in an economy can thus be expressed as:

C + I + G – S – T + (X – M).

So if a government wants to increase the country's overall domestic economic income, it can do so by:

- Trying to increase consumer spending (C)
- Trying to increase private investment (I)
- Increasing government spending (G)
- Reducing taxation (T)
- Trying to improve the balance of payments on overseas trade (X – M)

Economic growth

2.5 Economic growth may be measured by an annual percentage increase in the gross national product (GNP) or gross domestic product (GDP) per head of the population. Both of these terms are essentially measures of the level of output produced by the national economy. In the long run, this depends on:

- Demand factors: the total amount spent on domestic goods and services in the economy (aggregate demand) and
- Supply factors: the total potential output of the economy. A growth in capacity may be possible if more or better resources become available (eg more skilled workers, or the discovery of mineral deposits), or if ways are found of using resources more productively (eg through technological development, flexible labour practices or investment in infrastructure).

2.6 The main advantage of economic growth should be a better standard of living for the population as a whole. Greater output capacity should also mean a need for more inputs, increasing purchasing activity. However, there are also disadvantages to growth, including the faster usage of scarce natural resources (pushing up energy costs, for example) and more pollution and waste products: both of these effects may need to be managed by purchasing functions.

Interest rates

2.7 Interest is the amount of money charged by a lender to a borrower for the use of a loan. The 'base rate' (typically set by the government or the central bank) establishes the key interest rate in the economy.

2.8 The key point about interest rates is that as interest rates *rise,* the costs of *borrowing* increase (because borrowers are charged interest) – but so do the rewards for *saving* (because savings accounts earn interest). Either way, looking at our equation for total spending in an economy, as interest rates rise, economic activity is reduced; as they fall, it is increased. Governments therefore seek to manipulate interest rates to stimulate or slow down demand. This is a key aspect of **monetary policy**: the government's decisions and actions regarding the level of interest rates and the money supply.

2.9 The impact of an interest rate rise for purchasing will be, indirectly, a slow-down in demand for goods – and therefore a reduced need for inputs. In addition, if purchasing activities depend on borrowed funds (as they might do in the case of a major capital purchase, say), there would be a direct impact on costs. A reduction in the base rate would have the opposite effect.

Inflation

2.10 Inflation is a general, sustained increase in prices over time. This may be the result of:

- Demand for goods exceeding supply, pushing prices up (demand-pull inflation)
- Increases in the costs of production, particularly wages, without increased demand, so that producers have to raise their prices to maintain profitability (cost-push inflation)
- Overexpansion of the monetary supply, which boosts excessive demand by making more money available to spend (monetary inflation).

2.11 Once rates of inflation begin to increase, people may fear further price rises and seek higher wages and prices to cover them – creating 'expectational' inflation and a vicious circle called a 'wage-price spiral'. Inflation thus becomes persistent – even if the conditions which caused it are no longer present – because people *expect* it to occur and react accordingly.

2.12 A high rate of inflation is undesirable for a number of reasons. It disadvantages those on lower (and particularly, fixed) incomes, since their spending power is reduced. It causes uncertainty about the future value of money, which makes it harder for businesses to evaluate future expenditure, or the real value of large-scale capital items over their lifetime, or the likely return on investments: this may act as a disincentive to investment and long-term decision-making. In international trade, if the rate of inflation is higher in the UK than in other economies, exports become relatively expensive and imports relatively cheap: the balance of trade, and local employment, will suffer.

2.13 The control of inflation has therefore been a major policy objective in most developed nations since the 1970s. Strategies vary according to the contributory factors (and different economic theories).

2.14 Demand-pull inflation can be reduced by 'slowing down' the economy with measures such as the following.

- Reduced government spending
- Higher taxation to cut consumer spending (fiscal policy)
- Raising interest rates, increasing the costs of borrowing for both consumer and business spending (monetary policy).

2.15 Cost-push inflation can be managed by government intervention to reduce production costs and limit price rises. This can be done by:

- Applying controls over wage and price rises (prices and incomes policy)
- Encouraging increased productivity in industry (eg by funding technology development)

2.16 Monetary inflation can be controlled by limiting the money supply (monetary policy) in various ways:

- Trying to control or reduce bank lending
- Maintaining interest rates at a level that might encourage people to take their money out of the supply by increasing their savings
- Trying to achieve a balance of trade surplus (more exports than imports)

2.17 However, this still leaves substantial problems if the underlying cause of inflation is an increase in the cost of significant imported raw materials, such as oil, say.

Employment

2.18 The creation and maintenance of employment is a key focus of government economic policy, because – as we saw in Figure 6.1 – the flow of economic resources depends on wage income flowing into households (and out again in consumer spending).

2.19 High unemployment is undesirable for a number of reasons. Unemployed workers do not produce anything, making the total national income less than it could be. They may also lose their skills over time, through lack of use, creating a loss of productive capacity, and incurring costs of retraining. Rising unemployment is costly for governments because it means less tax (on income and spending) coming in – and more financial assistance benefits going out. And, of course, unemployment has personal and social costs: personal hardship and distress, and possibly knock-on effects such as increased crime and family breakdown.

2.20 Various types of unemployment have been identified.

- **Frictional unemployment** occurs where there is a shortage of a particular type of worker in one region, but a surplus in another. Surplus workers are therefore temporarily unemployed, for the time it takes for them to find a new job.
- **Seasonal unemployment** occurs in some industries, such as construction, farming and tourism, because the demand for workers fluctuates in seasonal cycles.
- **Structural unemployment** occurs where an industry undergoes long-term changes which result in lower demand for workers: the automation of mining and construction are two clear examples.
- **Cyclical unemployment** occurs when (as we will see below), industries or economies periodically go through times of decline and recession: the demand for output falls, and so does the demand for workers.

2.21 Governments can try to create jobs and/or to reduce unemployment in various ways. They may themselves create jobs and recruit more people into the public sector, or may encourage growth in the private sector of the economy. They may support education and training in vocational skills (or retraining, to combat structural unemployment), and job search or outplacement services (to reduce frictional unemployment).

3 The business cycle

'Boom and bust'

3.1 The business cycle (or trade cycle) is the periodic fluctuation in levels of economic activity, output and employment: from 'boom' to 'bust' (and back again). The understanding of business cycles can be crucial for purchasing, especially investment in capital goods like plant and machinery: this represents a hefty up-front expense in the anticipation of future returns (extra production capacity and sales revenue) – which may be at risk if the sector is hit by a downturn in demand due to the business cycle.

3.2 There are four main phases in a typical business cycle: Table 6.1

Table 6.1 *Phases in the business cycle*

Depression	There is low consumer demand; production capacity is unused; prices are stable or falling; business profits are low; there is high unemployment; and business confidence is low.
Recovery	Consumer spending rises; investment picks up; prices are stable or rising; profits and employment start to rise; and confidence grows.
Boom	Consumer spending is rising fast. Production capacity is reached, and there are labour shortages, so output can only be increased by new investment in labour-saving technology: investment spending is high. Increased demand stimulates price rises, and business profits are high.
Recession	Consumption starts to fall off; production falls; unemployment starts to rise; profits fall and some businesses fail; many investments suddenly become unprofitable and new investment falls.

3.3 Wide fluctuations in economic activity may damage the overall economic wellbeing of society – through the inflation and risk-taking of the booms, as well as the high unemployment of the busts. Governments generally seek to stabilise the economic system, trying to avoid extremes.

3.4 Purchasers may, however, need to anticipate and adapt resourcing decisions to suit each stage of the cycle. Here are some examples.

- Investment, purchasing and stock control decisions should be tailored to the anticipated level of demand (lower in a downturn and recession, and higher again in recovery).
- Costs may need to be reduced to cope with recessionary phases, particularly if the firm has to reduce the price of products and services in order to stimulate demand and maintain sales.
- Recruitment may need to be suspended in advance of recession, to allow the workforce to be reduced by natural wastage rather than redundancies. In highly cyclical industries, companies might be more proactive in developing a numerically flexible workforce (eg by subcontracting and outsourcing) – to which purchasing may contribute.

3.5 It is worth noting that forecasting the pattern and timing of the business cycle is very difficult in practice. The cycle is affected by complex factors such as oil prices, international political stability and the performance of other economies. The effects of the US mortgage lending ('sub prime') crisis, for example, precipitated a global financial crisis and warnings of recession towards the end of 2008.

The Budget

3.6 The Annual Budget is the overall report on the government's finances for a given year: its expenditure (public spending) and receipts (mainly from taxation) – and its estimate of the gap between them. This shortfall is the combined deficits of central government, local authorities and public corporations.

3.7 In times of recession, when unemployment is high, the government's tax take is low, as incomes and expenditures fall. Furthermore, government expenditure is high, as more people claim financial assistance from the state. So there will probably be a budget deficit, and the government will have to borrow funds to cover its obligations. The **national debt** is simply the accumulated government debt that has been run up (and not repaid) by year after year of deficits. During periods of economic boom, rising incomes and expenditure increase the tax take, benefit payouts fall, and the government may be able to pay back some of the national debt.

3.8   **Fiscal policy** is the term for policies aimed at managing the relationship between taxation and public spending.

- A government may seek to operate with a budget deficit (spending more than it receives in tax revenue), in order to stimulate total spending in the economy. Higher public sector spending should also have positive 'spin-off' effects, such as improved infrastructure (roads and so on). However, a high PSBR (large government borrowings) may force up interest rates and act as a disincentive to private sector investment in the economy, by making it too expensive for firms to borrow and invest profitably.
- Alternatively, a government may seek to operate with a budget surplus (spending less than it receives in tax revenue), in order to slow down total spending in the economy and bring inflation under control.

3.9   It is worth noting that this either/or view (held by Keynesian economists) is hotly contested by monetarist economists, who argue that government's role is to run a 'balanced budget': no deficit or surplus.

4   International economics

4.1   The main features of the international economic environment that will affect purchasing are as follows.

- The need to balance the flows of exports from and imports to the national economy (for reasons which will be discussed below). Measures intended to do this will affect the attractiveness of purchasing imported supplies.
- The policies of international trading blocs and partners in regard to protecting domestic producers (protectionism) or liberalising trade.
- The need to manage risks arising from exchange rates: that is, the price of one currency expressed in terms of another currency.

The balance of payments

4.2   The balance of payments is the statistical accounting record of all a country's external trade dealings in a given period (usually a year). It records the flows of value/money, rather than goods: imports are recorded as negative amounts (debits), as money is leaving the country to pay for the goods, while exports are recorded as positive amounts (credits), as money is coming into the country to pay for the goods.

4.3   These flows include:

- *Current transactions*, or payments for goods and services. The current account is subdivided into 'visible trade' (import and export of goods) and 'invisible trade' (import and export of services, interest, profits, dividends and money transfers). The balance of incoming and outgoing flows in visible trade is called the 'balance of trade' and the balance in current transactions overall is called the 'current balance'.
- *Capital transactions,* or flows of funds for investment purposes: long-term transactions such as the purchase of shares or real estate, or inter-government loans; and short-term transactions such as trade credit and foreign currency borrowing and lending.

Balance of payments surplus and deficit

4.4 A 'balance of payments surplus' usually refers to a balance on the current account where the value of exports is greater than the value of imports. A 'balance of payments deficit' refers to a balance on the current account where the value of imports is greater than the value of exports.

- A persistent *surplus* sounds good, but can cause problems. It may create excessive demand – greater than total domestic supply – putting upward pressure on prices. Moreover, one country's surplus is another's deficit, and the exporter may find its trade subject to tariffs or other import controls.
- A persistent *deficit* creates more severe problems. Since it represents a leakage of income from the national economy, it may erode growth. It is also likely to force exchange rates down, which will make the price of imports higher in domestic terms: this will have a clear implication for purchasers importing goods, as well as creating price inflation.

4.5 Governments can use a number of measures to reduce a balance of payments deficit (which is the bigger problem). The aims will be straightforward.

- To *increase exports* eg by giving support, information or financial subsidies to exporters, and/ or
- To *reduce imports* eg through trade restrictions or protectionism: import quotas, controls or tariffs (taxes on imports, which give a cost/price advantage to domestic producers of the same goods). This may not be possible, however, under EU rules or WTO treaty obligations.

4.6 Another approach will be to devalue the currency, lowering the exchange rate, and making exports cheaper and imports more expensive in domestic terms – as we will explain in the next section of the chapter.

Trading blocs

4.7 A trading bloc is an economic arrangement created among a group of countries. There are more than 30 trading organisations and blocs around the world, including: ASEAN (The Association of Southeast Asian Nations); EFTA (The European Free Trade Agreement); and NAFTA (the North American Free Trade Agreement). Trade *within* each of these three major trading blocs is expanding on a vast scale – while trading *between* blocs, or indeed with non-members, tends to decline.

4.8 Unlike the European Union, which has moved towards political integration, most trading blocs are solely about **economic integration**. This type of integration can take various forms.

- A **free-trade area** (such as EFTA and NAFTA) represents the least restrictive economic integration between nations. Essentially, in a free-trade area all barriers to trade among members are removed, and no discriminatory taxes, tariffs or quotas are imposed.
- A **common market** (such as the Andean Common Market – Ancom – comprising Venezuela, Columbia, Ecuador, Peru and Bolivia) is the closest form of integration: a trading group with tariff-free trade among members *and* a common external tariff on imports from non-members, *and* collective regulation on quotas and other non-tariff barriers. Commercial law is also drafted centrally, and overrides the domestic laws of member states.

Tariff and non-tariff barriers to trade

4.9 Outside trading blocs, international trade may be subject to barriers in the form of taxes and duties (tariffs) and non-tariff measures. Here are some examples.

- Quotas: limits on the quantities of specified products that are allowed to be imported
- Complex customs procedures and paperwork, for goods to cross borders
- The need to comply with different quality, health and safety, environmental protection and other regulations in different countries
- Government subsidies to domestic producers (which make it more difficult for overseas firms to compete on price)
- Exchange controls: limits on the ability of a domestic importer to obtain the foreign currency needed to pay his overseas suppliers.

4.10 However the trend – supported by bodies such as the World Trade Organisation – is to remove such barriers and to encourage free trade and competition.

5 Exchange rates

What are exchange rates?

5.1 As we noted earlier, the exchange rate is the price of a currency (say, pounds sterling or euros) expressed in terms of another currency (say, US dollars).

5.2 The exchange rate between two currencies is determined by the relative supply and demand for each currency.

- Demand for pound sterling may rise, for example, when foreign buyers need to pay for UK exports; or foreign investors want to invest in the UK (perhaps because interest rates are attractively high); or speculators want to buy sterling on the foreign exchange market, in the anticipation that its value is rising.
- Conversely, supply of sterling will rise when people sell their pounds in exchange for foreign currencies: UK residents wishing to buy imports or invest abroad, say, or speculators selling sterling in anticipation of the value falling.

5.3 If demand for a currency, relative to supply, is rising (eg if there is a balance of payments surplus: more exports than imports), the foreign exchange markets will tend to quote the currency at a higher exchange rate. If supply is rising, relative to demand (eg if there is a balance of payments deficit: more imports than exports), the exchange rate will tend to be lower.

5.4 Exchange rates which are left to be determined by supply and demand on the foreign exchange (forex) markets, without government intervention, are called 'freely floating' exchange rates. Exchange rates which are subject to occasional government intervention to prevent unwanted fluctuations or changes are called 'managed floating' exchange rates.

The impact of exchange rates

5.5 Exchange rates are important for firms in international product or supply markets.

5.6 *Importers* want the value of their currency to be as *high* as possible. If the value of sterling is strong or rising against a foreign currency, UK purchasers can acquire more of that currency to pay their foreign suppliers: imports will be cheaper in domestic terms. If sterling weakens, purchasers' ability to acquire overseas currency is reduced, and imports are more expensive in domestic terms. This is the major consideration for purchasers.

5.7   For *exporters*, the position is reversed. They want the value of their currency to be as *low* as possible. If the value of sterling is low against a foreign currency, overseas purchasers will be able to buy more pounds to pay for UK goods: UK exports will be more affordable to overseas purchasers. If the value of sterling is high, UK goods will be more expensive to foreign buyers, and UK suppliers will find it harder to compete with other international suppliers (with weaker currencies). They may be forced to reduce their selling price, with an adverse effect on profits.

5.8   Firms producing goods for the domestic market *in competition with foreign imports* similarly want the value of sterling to be *low*, as this makes imports more expensive in domestic terms, favouring domestic suppliers. If sterling rises, imports will be more competitive.

5.9   *Fluctuations in foreign exchange rates* therefore represent a source of financial *risk* for purchasing organisations. An overseas supplier will normally quote a price in its own currency, and the buyer will need to purchase currency in order to make payment. If sterling weakens between the time when the price is agreed and the purchase of the currency, the buyer will end up paying more. The risk is even greater if staged payments are to be made.

Managing exchange rate risk

5.10   There are a number of ways of managing exchange rate risk.

- The purchaser might be able to transfer the risk to the suppliers, by getting them to quote prices in sterling. (This might be a tough negotiation, unless the purchaser has strong power in the relationship, or can offer concessions in exchange.)
- If fluctuations are not extreme, it may be possible to estimate the rate that will apply at the time of payment, and negotiate prices accordingly (perhaps with a contract proviso that prices will be *re*-negotiated if the exchange rate fluctuates by a stated percentage or reaches a stated rate).
- It may be possible to agree to pay for the goods at the time of contract (ie at a known exchange rate), without waiting for delivery – although this creates another kind of risk.
- Another approach would be to use one of the available tools of currency management, such as a **forward exchange contract**. Under this arrangement, the organisation contracts now to purchase the overseas currency at a stated future date, at a rate of exchange agreed now. There is a cost to doing this, but the uncertainty is removed.
- If exchange rate risks are severe, a purchaser may consider sourcing from the domestic market, from a single currency market such as the EU, or from other markets with less volatile currencies. (We will examine the economics of international sourcing briefly below.)

The single currency

5.11   One of the long-standing objectives of the EU has been 'monetary union' or a single currency area. The euro became general currency within the EU in 2002, although some member states (including the UK) opted to keep their own currencies. In other members, euro notes and coins replaced the old national notes and coins, such as the Deutschmark in Germany and the franc in France. The establishment of the euro irrevocably fixed exchange rates between participants' currencies.

5.12 The argument still rages as to whether the UK should join the single currency and adopt the euro. The arguments for and against are summarised in Table 6.2.

Table 6.2 *Arguments for and against the UK adopting the euro*

ARGUMENTS FOR A SINGLE CURRENCY	ARGUMENTS AGAINST A SINGLE CURRENCY
Greater stability of economic policy	Loss of control over economic policy
Facilitating trade and investment, without the risks and costs of currency transactions	The need to 'bail out' weaker economies in order to hold the system together
Currency stability, enabling lower interest rates for borrowing	Cost and confusion in moving to a new currency and coinage
Preserving the City of London's position as a premier financial market	Lower confidence arising from loss of national pride
Transparency of transactions, wage and price comparisons	

5.13 At the time of writing (Summer 2012) the euro faces a crisis arising from deep-seated financial problems in countries such as Greece, and for the foreseeable future it is unlikely that the UK will change its current stance on the issue.

6 The economics of international sourcing

6.1 It may be worth drawing together some of the key economic factors impacting on a purchaser's decision on whether to source from international suppliers.

6.2 Overseas economies may have lower costs of production (labour costs, environmental compliance costs), which can be passed on to purchasers as lower prices. This is the overwhelming reason why companies now source internationally, or outsource production to low-labour-cost countries. However, there is increasing pressure for buyers not to *exploit* overseas workers, with an emphasis on Fair Trading (fair prices paid to suppliers) and ethical monitoring of suppliers (to ensure that their workers have fair terms and conditions).

6.3 International sourcing will incur additional costs of: procurement staff training and systems preparation; larger order and stock quantities (because of longer lead times for delivery); transport and logistics; compliance (with different laws and regulatory regimes); transport and exchange rate risk (and risk management: insurances, forward contracts and so on); contracting and payment (given the complexity and distance); supplier selection and monitoring; quality assurance; and so on. Low prices are only one part of the total purchasing cost.

6.4 International trade is often subject to trade restrictions or protectionist measures, in the form of taxes and duties (tariffs) and non-tariff measures, including quotas, customs red tape, legal requirements, government subsidies for domestic producers and exchange controls. However, these are being reduced with increasing trade liberalisation, particularly within trading blocs such as EU or ASEAN.

6.5 Additional risk is posed by the fact that economic factors are constantly changing, and international factors may be harder to predict. As an example, consider the troubles facing organisations that source from (or outsource to) China at the moment.

- Economists forecast that the over-supply of cheap Chinese labour will not last much longer: annual wage increases of 15% will soon erode its cost advantage.
- The introduction of new labour laws at the beginning of 2008 may also increase costs in China.
- Changes in Chinese tax regulations may affect Chinese suppliers' ability to reclaim VAT on some commodities (including chemicals, clothes, metals and machinery) – and the costs may be passed up the supply chain to international buyers.

Chapter summary

- Macro-economic factors affect buyers in a number of ways: by influencing the amount of disposable income; by influencing the level of business confidence; by influencing employment levels, rates of inflation, rates of taxation, exchange rates and interest rates.

- Economic activity can be shown as a flow of resources between firms and households. Refinements to the basic model take account of injections to the system (investment spending, government spending) and withdrawals from the system (savings, taxation), as well as the level of net imports and exports.

- The national micro-economic environment includes factors such as: economic activity and growth; employment; inflation; taxation; interest rates; business cycles; and government intervention via monetary and fiscal policy. Each of these areas may have an impact on purchasing by affecting demand, costs and risk.

- The business cycle (or trade cycle) is the periodic fluctuation in levels of economic activity, output and employment: from 'boom' to 'bust' and back again. Buyers may need to adapt resourcing decisions to suit each stage of the cycle.

- The main features of the international economic environment are: the balance of payments (and government action to increase exports and/or decrease imports); and exchange rates (which affect the price of imports and demand for exports). International sourcing has both economic benefits and costs and risks.

- Buyers must increasingly consider whether to source from abroad. Overseas economies may have lower costs of production. However, there are additional costs to be considered as well: training staff, systems preparation etc. In addition, there are risks associated with international purchasing that do not apply to domestic sourcing (eg unpredictable political and economic fluctuations).

Self-test questions

Numbers in brackets refer to paragraphs where you can check your answers

1   Distinguish between macro- and micro-economics (Introduction)

2   Distinguish between monetary policy and fiscal policy. (1.3)

3   Explain the circular flow of national income. (2.3–2.4)

4   How might a rise in interest rates affect a business? (2.9)

5   List three causes of inflation and how they can be controlled. (2.10, 2.11, 2.14–2.16)

6   Describe the four phases in the business cycle. (3.2)

7   Explain the effect on UK importers of a balance of payments deficit. (4.4)

8   Explain the effect on UK importers of a rise in the value of sterling against the currency of the supplier's country. (5.6)

9   List three ways of managing exchange rate risk. (5.10)

10   What are the economic arguments for and against international sourcing? (6.2ff)

CHAPTER 7

Political Factors

Assessment criteria and indicative content

3.3 Explain the implications of political and legislative criteria that impact on procurement and supply

- Political criteria such as stability and instability that impact on organisations, different economic sectors and on countries

Section headings

1. The political environment
2. Local politics
3. National politics
4. Government policy and funding
5. International politics and policies

Introduction

In this chapter, we continue our more detailed survey of the STEEPLE factors which make up the wider macro environment of organisations.

We suggested in Chapter 5 that the STEEPLE factors should not be too strictly compartmentalised, because they are all interrelated: as we will see in this chapter, for example, economic factors are the subject of manipulation and management by political forces and bodies. Similarly, political forces are shaped by social and cultural values – and are often applied via legislative or legal measures. Nevertheless, it is worth distinguishing each of the STEEPLE factors for the purposes of analysis, especially since exam questions may ask you to focus on one area of the purchasing environment – and the assessors will expect you to know what issues and elements 'belong' to a discussion of each area.

In this chapter, we start by giving an overview of the political environment and how it affects business. We then explore local and national (UK) political structures and processes in more detail: obviously, if you are studying in a country outside the UK, you will be able to use your knowledge of your own political system.

Finally, we turn our attention to the 'supra-national' level of politics, looking at the purpose and impact of international political bodies on business.

1 The political environment

What is politics?

1.1 *Politics* is, broadly, a term for the processes through which power and influence are applied to handle conflicts of interest between stakeholders. (This is the sense in which we talk about 'office politics', for example, or 'gender politics'.) More commonly, it refers to these processes at the level of the State: the ways in which stakeholder interests are harmonised – for example, through competing political parties offering alternative policies and ideologies, the activity of pressure groups, democratic elections, the role of government in making decisions on society's behalf, and the way in which laws and regulations are formulated and enacted.

Overview of how political factors affect business

1.2   Political factors affect businesses in a variety of ways.

- Local government authorities formulate policies and bye-laws which affect local infrastructure, use of land and buildings, and service delivery.
- At a national level, the political process includes *legislation* (which directly affects business activity) and the *economic policy* of governments (which influences prices, labour availability, consumer spending, borrowing costs and other important factors of business).
- The government controls much of the economy, as the nation's largest supplier, employer, customer and investor: policy shifts can transform markets. (Think about the defence and aerospace industries, say.)
- As businesses increasingly trade in international markets, the politics of other nations (such as government policy or political instability in an overseas supplier's or subcontractor's country) also create opportunities and risks.
- Political influences cross national boundaries: eg through international institutions such as the European Union (whose directives affect all member countries) and the World Trade Organisation.
- Businesses are influenced *by* political factors – but they also exert some influence *over* them (or seek to do so): by lobbying government decision makers, making financial donations to political parties, influencing public opinion and so on.

1.3   The impact of political factors on a given business will vary according to the type of organisation involved: whether its market is local, national or multi-national; whether it operates in the public or private sector, or in a highly-regulated or de-regulated industry; and so on. We will, inevitably, make some generalisations in this chapter, but you will need to think carefully about which factors apply, and how, in the case of your own organisation, or in regard to an organisation described in the exam.

1.4   In general, however, the likelihood of political change (particularly in democratic systems) complicates management's task of predicting future environmental influences and planning to meet them. Some political changes cannot easily be planned for.

2   Local politics

Local or 'sub-national' government

2.1   Local government authorities represent democratic self-government by and for the people of a locality. Authorities have a wide range of responsibilities.

- Determining policy and rules (bye-laws), and applying national laws within their areas. This will affect business in various ways: planning regulations might influence business growth, or the siting of warehouse facilities; environmental health policy may affect logistics and storage (eg of foodstuffs or dangerous goods).
- Raising funds (via council tax and business rates, and any revenue raised by municipal enterprises) and allocating funds provided by central government and regional bodies in the

form of grants. Business will be directly affected by business rates, as a cost – and by business grants and tax relief, as a source of finance.

- Administering local authority services, such as housing, social services, education, environmental health, refuse collection, libraries and (on a discretionary basis) sport and leisure services. Some of these services may be contracted out to – or operated in competition with – private sector businesses. Each will have its own procurement needs, and may be a significant player in the local supply market.

Drivers and initiatives in local politics

2.2 A number of *initiatives* (proposals for change) and *drivers* (pressures for change) have recently affected the sub-national political environment, some of which have significant implications for purchasing. The following are just some relevant examples: you may wish to gather your own examples from the website, mailings and activities of your own local council.

2.3 Local government is facing pressures to reform its decision-making processes, which will affect how businesses deal with local bodies.

2.4 Sustainability (including sustainable procurement) has become a policy priority, driven by central government guidelines, academic research and public pressure. The London Borough of Camden recently appointed a sustainable procurement manager, for example, and changed its policies in areas such as the following.

- Environmental sustainability: increasing the use of environmental products and saving energy (eg recycled paper, recycled aggregate for highway maintenance)
- Social sustainability: ensuring that the workforce reflects the diversity of the area; using local and small business suppliers; supporting the use of local labour and the long-term unemployed; re-contracting school meal provision for more healthy nutrition; and so on.

2.5 Procurement efficiency has also become a policy priority, driven by central government efficiency guidelines and financial imperatives (the need to cut costs in order to improve stakeholder value). Many councils are pooling their procurement on a regional or category basis, for example, in order to gain economies of scale through consolidated buying. Others are developing or joining shared electronic procurement systems.

3 National politics

Branches of national government

3.1 National government consists of three branches.

- The *legislature,* which represents the people between elections, and makes the country's laws. In the UK, this function is carried out by Parliament: a non-elected House of Lords and an elected House of Commons (made up of MPs from a range of political parties). Proposed legislation ('bills') are passed through both houses, before they receive the assent of the reigning monarch and become 'Acts' of Parliament.
- The *executive,* which implements law and policy in practice. In the UK, this function is carried out by the Cabinet and non-Cabinet ministers (assisted by the Civil Service), committees, government departments, local authorities and quangos.
- An independent *judiciary* (judges and the courts), which enforces the laws enacted by Parliament and interprets European Union law.

Drivers and initiatives in national politics

3.2   Democratic systems are inevitably dynamic, because of the potential for the nation to change governments (with regular elections), and for government to change policies (with pressure group influence and new information). Some of the key changes at the national level, with relevance for purchasing, include the following.

- A broad political consensus on the value of market-based policies (previously identified only with right-wing politics), as a way of achieving employment, tax revenue and 'trickle down' prosperity to benefit all social stakeholders. This has contributed, for example, to new possibilities for partnership between private and public sector firms – as discussed above.
- Increasing internationalisation of social and environmental policy: eg commitments to enact EU directives into UK law, or commitment to Kyoto Agreement targets.
- Proposals to reform the political system (eg the House of Lords, the civil service, new voting systems and new policy-making and delivery systems) – which will alter the relationship between business and government bodies.
- Changing government policy, reflected in legislation, public sector guidelines and funding priorities. The news throws up new examples every day, but you might be able to think of some from recent years such as new legislation on age discrimination in employment, government initiatives on education and skilling (eg UfI, the University for Industry), or increased funding for the health sector. Specifically in the field of purchasing, there have been initiatives on sustainable procurement, procurement efficiency, and the Public Contracts Regulations.
- Increased use of technology in government-to-citizen and government-to-business communication – including public sector take-up of e-procurement systems.

3.3   Again, it will be beneficial for you to scan the quality press and government websites to gather your own relevant and up-to-date examples of government initiatives and policy drivers, as they change with national and international events. A classic example is the pressure caused by the threat of global economic recession, emerging towards the end of 2008: panic in the share markets; the threatened collapse and bailing out of major financial service providers; public demand to secure investments (coupled with outrage at a taxpayer funded 'bail-out' of the financial sector); and so on. How – and how effectively – has the national government (both parliament and Cabinet) responded to these pressures? What party-political or ideological factors have influenced the response from different political stakeholders?

Political parties

3.4   Political parties are major players in politics, because it is from them – in a democratic system – that a government is selected (by virtue of having the most members of parliament). A political party is likely to have a position on a variety of public policy areas, as a platform on which to stand for election – and these positions, and the ideologies underlying them, are a strong influence on the decisions of the party in power. In addition, the minority parties in parliament (the Opposition) provide checks and balances on government power, through public debate and voting on proposed legislation.

3.5   *The media* is another key influencer, with its potential to exert pressure on government (and also business) by arousing or reflecting public opinion.

Pressure groups and interest groups

3.6 *Interest groups* (representing a particular group of stakeholders) and *pressure groups* (promoting a particular issue or cause) also seek to influence government and public opinion in the areas of their interests. Some of these groups may employ professional *lobbyists* to seek to influence government decision-makers.

3.7 Causal pressure groups seek to promote a cause or issue: to raise awareness, mobilise opinion and lobby for changes in government policy or regulation. Examples include: political and human rights groups (such as the Campaign for Nuclear Disarmament or Amnesty International); environmental groups (such as Greenpeace or Friends of the Earth); and social welfare groups (such as Fair Trade, Oxfam, or the Royal Society for the Blind).

3.8 Such groups may seek to influence both government (via lobbying and mobilising public opinion) and businesses whose policies or practices they disagree with (via mobilising consumers to choose alternative products and services). You might therefore add them to the list of potential stakeholders of an organisation. As part of the political process, government and firms may seek to co-opt influential pressure groups to provide advice on their areas of expertise – or to support and collaborate on initiatives (eg a firm getting Fair Trade certification for its brands, or getting the public endorsement of Greenpeace for its environmental policy).

3.9 Sectional pressure groups (or interest groups) seek to promote or defend the interest of particular stakeholders in society.

3.10 Many workers are represented by **trade unions** relevant to their industry or occupation (such as the National Union of Teachers in the UK). Trade unions mainly seek to protect their members' rights and interests at work, through their collective power in negotiation with employers. They typically focus on fair pay, benefits and conditions; fair treatment (eg in relation to dismissal from a job); access to information and consultation on issues affecting their work or livelihoods (eg notice of redundancies); access to training and development opportunities; and the right to pursue individual and collective disputes with an employer. However, they also provide funding for political parties, and have traditionally been a strong influence on the policy of the Labour Party, in particular.

3.11 Business firms are represented in the political process by **employer associations** and **trade associations**, which promote the economic interests of commercial organisations, and are often given a key role in industry policy formation and implementation.

3.12 Pressure groups, as part of the broader political scene, may influence organisations in a number of ways. They may influence corporate strategy (eg introducing Fair Trade brands or environmental policies); create pressure or opportunities to develop new products (eg recyclable products, animal-friendly cosmetics) or modify business processes (eg product recycling or supplier ethical monitoring). Firms may also seek to ally or associate themselves with pressure groups which reflect their values, or those of their customers, in order to gain their support and endorsement.

4 Government policy and funding

Government influence on business

4.1 Some state intervention in economic activity is justified by the need to distribute resources fairly, to regulate the private sector in the public interest, and to correct market failures, ensuring that the factors of production are used in the interests of all citizens.

4.2 The government may influence business activity through a number of mechanisms.

- Economic policy (eg on taxation, inflation and interest rates), which affects investment and market demand – as we will see later in this chapter
- Industry policy (eg protection of domestic producers from imported competition; grants, incentives and sponsorships; and industry regulation) which affects costs and methods of doing business
- Environment and infrastructure policy (eg investment in roads and telecommunications, and environmental protection regulations) which supports – or constrains – business processes
- Social policy (eg education and skills training, workplace regulation and employment law) which affects the availability, quality, cost and management of human resources
- Foreign policy (eg trade promotion, support for exports, EU and World Trade Organisation obligations)
- Public spending on goods and services (the State in its role as buyer) and provision of goods and services (the State in its role as supplier), which generate significant economic activity in themselves.

4.3 Government policy is itself influenced by a variety of factors: party ideology, existing commitments, available and projected future resources, promises made to voters, and the political influence of the kinds of groups discussed earlier. Political influence is particularly important, as it provides a system of 'checks and balances' to curb government influence and protect stakeholder interests.

National government funding

4.4 Grants for *private* sector businesses are available from a huge variety of sources, many of them connected with government institutions. Tracking availability of grants is so complicated that specialist consultancies exist to advise businesses whether they qualify for any kind of grant assistance. They might do so, for instance, if they operate in geographical regions where the government is attempting to stimulate employment. Or they might be engaged in research and development work into scientific areas which the government wishes to encourage.

4.5 Of course, the government also provides primary funding for *public* sector services: schools, hospitals, the police force and so on. Both local and central government raise funds to finance the projects and services for which they are responsible. By far the largest element of public finance is raised from taxation. The central government raises tax revenue from both direct taxes (income tax, national insurance contributions, corporation tax, capital gains tax and so on) and indirect taxes (such as VAT and excise duties).

5 International politics and policies

The European Union (EU)

5.1 Decisions, law and policy affecting business activity are increasingly being made at a supra-national ('above national') level, through political and trading 'blocs' and agreements. We will examine some of the main international bodies briefly: other issues, such as economic integration and trade sanctions, are more relevant to the economic environment, and will be discussed in the following chapter.

5.2 In Europe, a Common Market was set up in 1957 by the Treaty of Rome, to support free mobility of goods, services, labour and capital across national boundaries: this was seen as being of paramount importance for the overall economic prosperity of the region. The Single European Market was formed in 1992 – and these advances developed further into much closer integration, signalled by the current title of European Union.

5.3 The political institutions of the EU include the following.

- The *European Commission* comprises one Commissioner from each member state (nominated by their governments), supported by a permanent civil service. Its role is: to propose policies and legislation; to implement EU policies and supervise their day-to-day running; and to ensure that EU Treaties are respected.
- The *Council of the European Union (Council of Ministers)* comprises one Minister from each of the member states (varying according to the issue under discussion eg Agriculture, Employment and Social Affairs, Economics and Finance). The council makes the major policy decisions and responds to legislative proposals put forward by the European Commission.
- The *European Parliament* is an assembly of directly elected members, representing each of the member states (in a proportion roughly equal to their populations). The parliament debates and approves legislation, prior to its formal adoption by the Council of Ministers; acts as the community's budgetary authority; supervises the European Commission; and initiates debate on issues requiring policy change.
- The *European Court of Justice* is designed to decide interpretations of EU law, and to quash any measures which conflict with EU Treaties.

5.4 EU policy has an important impact on business, and on purchasing in particular. The concept of economic union, for example, ensures that goods and capital can flow from one member state to another without barriers or trade restrictions (in the form of import quotas, tariffs or customs formalities): this facilitates cross-border supply and logistics. The adoption of a common currency (the euro) facilitates price comparisons and payments, while a common product protection regime (with a single patent office) minimises intellectual property risk.

5.5 Meanwhile, EU directives have influenced UK law on a range of business and employment issues such as working hours, health and safety, equal opportunity, competition and environmental protection.

5.6 The EU procurement directives (enacted in UK law as the Public Contracts and Public Utilities Regulations) provide that decisions on public procurement in the EU for contracts above a certain value must be based on value for money, obtained via competitive tender. The directives focus on areas such as non-discrimination in specifications, and the use of objective decision criteria.

7

Other regional blocs

5.7   Other regional blocs for the purposes of economic integration, in other parts of the world, include ASEAN (The Association of Southeast Asian Nations) and NAFTA (the North American Free Trade Agreement).

The World Trade Organisation (WTO)

5.8   The WTO (formerly the General Agreement on Tariffs and Trade, or GATT) is an organisation dedicated to promoting free trade between nations. Its main aim is to reduce or remove barriers to trade from tariffs (import taxes and duties) and non-tariff factors (eg quotas, customs red-tape, different regulatory regimes, foreign currency controls, and government subsidies to domestic producers). The usual reason for such barriers is to protect domestic (or trading bloc) industry from the effects of outside competition – a policy called *protectionism.* It is argued, however, that protectionism inhibits economic growth and leads to political ill will and retaliation between nations, stifling international trade.

5.9   The WTO contains high-level policy making councils and a number of subsidiary bodies, such as: the Disputes Settlement Body (which helps to settle trade disputes and breach of rules) and the Trade Policy Review Body (which, among other activities, publishes regular country reports on trade policies).

5.10   While critics argue that the WTO favours the interests of developed countries over developing ones, it has significant influence on purchasing in areas such as opening up markets, facilitating international sourcing and protecting intellectual property rights (designs, patents, copyright and so on).

The Organisation for Economic Co-operation and Development (OECD)

5.11   The OECD has its roots in co-operation to rebuild Western European economies after the Second World War. It comprises 30 members drawn from the richest and most advanced industrial countries in the world, and represents the main forum for their governments to get together to discuss economic matters. The focus is on supporting sustainable growth, free trade and economic development in less affluent non-member countries. The OECD has no direct authority to set policy, but exerts political influence through discussion, persuasion, and the publishing of economic data on member countries.

The Group of Eight (G8)

5.12   Representatives of the eight leading industrial economies (the USA, Japan, Germany, France, Italy, Canada, Britain and Russia) meet annually to discuss issues of mutual interest: human rights, economic management, the environment and so on. These Group of Eight (or G8) summits attract significant media attention – as well as opposition from anti-globalisation protestors!

Chapter summary

- Political factors include local government processes; national legislation and government policy; overseas government and trade policies; transnational political and economic structures (such as the EU, WTO, OECD and G8); and the interplay of influence between government, business and pressure groups and interest groups.
- There are a number of drivers (influences for change) and initiatives (proposals for change) in the political environment, and you should try to keep up to date with the changing scene.
- One form of political intervention is government funding, for both the private and public sector. Private-public-partnerships are a relatively new model, private sector involvement in the design, building, finance and/or operation of public works.
- Businesses are increasingly affected by supra-national bodies, such as the European Union, the World Trade Organisation, and the Organisation for Economic Co-operation and Development.

Self-test questions

Numbers in brackets refer to paragraphs where you can check your answers

1   Define 'politics' (1.1)

2   Give an example of local, national and international political factors impacting on business (1.2)

3   What is the role of local government authorities? (2.1)

4   Explain the roles of the three components of UK government. (3.1)

5   What is the role of political parties in the political environment? (3.4)

6   What are 'interest groups' and 'pressure groups', and how do they wield influence on the political scene? (3.6–3.12)

7   Give three examples of government policy that may impact on business. (4.2)

8   What are the main impacts on business of EU policy? (5.4)

9   What are the main impacts on business of the activities of the WTO? (5.8–5.10)

CHAPTER 8

Legal Factors

Assessment criteria and indicative content

3.3 Explain the implications of political and legislative criteria that impact on procurement and supply

- Legislation that impacts on organisations such as on standards, health and safety, environmental standards and employment law

Section headings

1. The sources of English law
2. Contracts and the sale of goods
3. Employment law
4. Equal opportunity
5. Health and safety at work
6. Other law affecting purchasing

Introduction

In this chapter we address the next of the STEEPLE factors: legislative influences impacting on procurement and supply.

Once again, it is difficult to say anything about this topic without citing specific examples of legal regulations, and in this Course Book we naturally focus on English law. If you live in a different legal system you may want to research examples from your local law to supplement your knowledge. But a word of caution: in the corresponding unit of the old (pre-2013 syllabus) the examiner frequently required knowledge of specifically English law. We understand that this will not be the case in future, but we are reluctant to guarantee it . . .

1 The sources of English law

The legal environment

1.1 In any community, some agreed rules are essential in order to be able to control the actions of individual citizens for the common good. 'Law' broadly consists of a body of rules laid down by society to regulate human conduct: if these rules are broken, penalties and other sanctions can be imposed. The broader 'legal environment' consists of legislation, regulations, voluntary codes of practice and other requirements formulated by governments (by enacting legislation or statutes), courts (by setting legal 'precedents' or case law) and regulatory bodies.

1.2 This is a particularly important area for environmental monitoring and purchasing management for the following reasons.

- The organisation's response is not 'optional' or left to managerial discretion: compliance is required and enforced by various sanctions and penalties

- The requirements are constantly changing, as courts and tribunals define them through their decisions, and as legislators and regulatory bodies issue new provisions and amendments
- Purchasing involves a number of activities which are the specific focus of law and regulation, including the development and fulfilment of contracts, the employment of staff, and competitive tendering (in the public sector).

1.3 The English legal system incorporates the law of England and Wales. (Within the UK both Scotland and Northern Ireland have different legal systems.) The law within this system derives from four main sources: common law, equity, statute law and EC law.

Common law

1.4 **Common law** is a body of law which applies throughout England and Wales. It consists of statements and interpretations of fundamental legal principles, declared by judges in the course of deciding legal disputes. Here are some examples.

- The common law principles of the **law of contract**: when contracts are validly formed; how contract terms should be interpreted; when contracts are terminated; and what remedies are available for breach of contract.
- The common law principles of **tort**: the set of rules that determine when one person must pay compensation to another for harm wrongfully caused, as a result of intentional malice, recklessness or negligence.

1.5 **Equity** is a similar collection of discretionary rules and remedies devised by judges to decide cases on the basis of fairness and good conscience, where the complexity and rigidity of common law might work against fair solutions.

1.6 Common law and equity can be grouped under the heading of **case law** (eg if an exam question specifies 'three sources of English law'). The doctrine of 'judicial precedent' states that when judges determine principles when making their decisions in legal disputes, those principles should be followed in similar later cases, where possible. Case law is the body of legal principles established by judges' decisions in previous cases. Legal cases are usually referred to in the form *Smith v Jones (200X)*: you will come across this formula often if you continue your studies into legal aspects of purchasing.

Statute law

1.7 **Statute law** is the law created by Parliament and its delegated bodies. Statutes (Acts of Parliament and other statutory instruments) are binding on everyone in the jurisdiction and supersede both the common law and equity. Examples include the Sex Discrimination Act 1975, the Freedom of Information Act 2000 and the Sale of Goods Act 1979. We will discuss a number of statutes relevant to purchasing in this chapter, since statute law is designed both:

- to codify and enforce the principles of *common law* on a particular matter; and
- to implement *European law* within the English legal system.

European Community (EC) law

1.8 It is common (though not invariable) to refer to EC law (rather than EU law), because the European Community is one of the 'three pillars' of the European Union, and is the one that gives rise to legislation. The Council of the EU and the European Commission exercise law-making powers that have an effect on the English legal system.

- *Regulations* are designed to achieve uniformity of law among the member states, and have direct force of law in all member states without the need for further legislation – even if legislation conflicts with them.
- *Directives* are designed to harmonise the law of member states, in the form of instructions to member states to bring their laws into line with EC law by a certain date. Examples include the Working Time Directive (implemented by the UK Working Time Regulations) and the Public Procurement Directive (implemented by the UK Public Contracts Regulations). There are EU directives on areas such as equal opportunity; privacy and data protection; environmental issues (including the Waste Electrical and Electronic Directive, or WEEE); intellectual property protection; and several other areas.

1.9 Perhaps the most obvious EU directive with an impact on purchasing is the Public Procurement Directive, and we will focus on this in our coverage. EU directives cannot be separated from statute law in many cases, because the EC law has been (or is being) implemented into UK statute: we will indicate where this is the case.

Civil and criminal law

1.10 It may also be helpful to know that there are two basic branches of English law.

- **Civil law** assists 'individuals' (including groups or organisations) to recover property or enforce obligations owed to them: eg in disputes over breach of contract, defamation, unfair dismissal or discrimination.
- **Criminal law** assists the State to suppress crime and to punish (and, theoretically, reform) offenders: eg cases of theft or murder.

1.11 In civil law, one individual, group or organisation (the claimant) sues another (the defendant) to obtain redress for some wrong, usually in the form of financial compensation (called damages). The court hearing, initially held in a county court or high court, is called litigation. Most legal cases relevant to purchasing will be of the civil type (eg disputes over contracts), although some breaches may constitute a criminal offence (eg fraud).

1.12 We will now look at some of the main areas of law affecting purchasing.

2   Contracts and the sale of goods

Common law in regard to contracts

2.1 A contract is an agreement between two or more parties which is intended to be enforceable by law. This is different from a social agreement, such as arranging to borrow a friend's car for the day: if one party does not carry out his part, he will not be taken to court by the other to enforce the agreement. However, if the agreement is between two commercial enterprises, it is *presumed* that there is an intention to 'enter into legal relations': that is, to use the law to enforce the agreement if necessary.

2.2 The law of contract is concerned with four basic questions.

- *Is there a contract in existence?* The answer depends on the presence of five essential elements: agreement (offer and acceptance); consideration (some form of exchange, eg payment of money for goods); intention to create legal relations; legal capacity to enter into contracts (eg being over 18 and of sound mind); and correct form (since *some* types of contract, such as share transfers and hire purchase agreements, must be in writing – although in general, oral agreements are binding if the other elements are present).

- *Is the agreement one which the law should recognise and enforce?* Some contracts will be wholly or partly unenforceable, because of undermining factors such as a mistake or misunderstanding in what a party thought he was agreeing to.
- *When do the obligations of the parties come to an end?* The most common method of terminating a contract is when both parties have performed their contractual obligations (ie the terms of the contract) to mutual satisfaction. However, contracts can also be terminated by the failure of one or both parties to meet an essential term of the contract ('breach of contract').
- *What remedies are available for the injured party if the other party fails to meet his obligations?* Possibilities include monetary compensation for the loss suffered (damages), or a court order for the other party to carry out his obligations.

2.3   In general, parties are at liberty (in common law) to make their own bargains, and the courts will not interfere with the terms they agree upon, as long as both parties clearly understand what those terms are. This is called 'freedom of contract'. (One reason why purchasers need to be careful when drawing up contracts: once you make an agreement, you will generally have to abide by it, unless you are released from your obligations by the other party.) However, there are some exceptions, which illustrate the intervening role of *statute law*.

- If the parties have failed to express all the terms of their agreement, the court may *imply* terms based on their presumed intentions. Sometimes, such terms are automatically implied by statute. For example, the Sale of Goods Act 1979 (discussed below) lays down implied terms which will apply to *all* contracts for the sale of goods – unless specifically excluded in the contract.
- Some types of contract clause may be *disallowed*, because they conflict with statutory principles. For example, clauses limiting the liability of a party (exclusion clauses) may not be allowable under the Unfair Contract Terms Act 1977, so that firms cannot disclaim responsibility for loss or harm suffered by consumers as a result of negligence, say.

The effect of case law

2.4   There is a vast body of case law defining how common law principles and statutory provisions are to be interpreted and enforced in different circumstances – and you will need to get to grips with key cases at later stages of your CIPS studies. To give you a flavour of how it works, however, we will cite a couple of examples.

2.5   We have said that for a valid contract to exist, there must be offer and acceptance. But what happens if an offer is withdrawn? In the case *Routledge v Grant (1828)*, Grant offered to buy Routledge's horse and gave him six weeks to decide whether or not to accept. Before the six weeks had elapsed Grant withdrew his offer. The dispute went to court, and the judge decided that since Routledge had not yet accepted, there was no contract, and Grant was entitled to withdraw the offer, even though he had stated that he would keep it open for a given time. Judges in similar cases will now adopt this precedent as a legal principle.

2.6   The Sale of Goods Act 1979 provides that if a buyer enters into a purchase contract based on a description of the goods, it is *implied* that the goods delivered should correspond to the description. If they don't, the buyer can reject the goods and refuse to pay for them. But how close to the description do the goods have to be? In *Moore v Landauer (1927)*, there was a contract for tinned fruit to be delivered packed in cases of 30 tins each. The correct number of tins was delivered – but in cases varying between 24 and 30 tins each. The judge held that the contract was not satisfactorily performed, even though the market value of the goods was the same: the buyer could reject all goods and not pay. Again, judges in similar cases now adopt this precedent as a legal principle, where possible.

The effect of statute: the Sale of Goods Act 1979

2.7 The Sale of Goods Act 1979 draws together the legal principles relating to contracts in which a seller transfers property (ownership or title) in goods to a buyer in exchange for a money consideration (price). Sections 12–15 of the Act set out terms which are *implied* into all contracts of sale of goods, principally to protect the buyer: Table 8.1.

Table 8.1 *The Sale of Goods Act*

S	IMPLIED TERM	EXPLANATION
12	**Title (ownership)**	The seller is deemed to undertake that he has a right to sell the goods (eg as a true owner of the goods, or without infringing a patent)
13	**Sale by description**	In a sale by description, the offer includes some description (specification and quantity of goods, time of delivery etc), on which the buyer relies in accepting. The seller is deemed to undertake that the goods will correspond with the description.
14	**Satisfactory quality and fitness for purpose**	Where the seller supplies goods in the course of a business, he is deemed to undertake that: • The goods will be of satisfactory quality: working and in good condition (so far as may be reasonably expected) and free from 'minor defects' (except defects drawn to the buyer's attention or which pre-contract inspection ought to have revealed) • The goods will be fit for the purpose for which they are commonly used, or for any specific purpose made known by the buyer to the seller
15	**Sale by sample**	Sale by sample occurs when the contract gives the buyer an opportunity to examine a small part of goods to be bought, as typical of the whole (bulk). The seller is deemed to undertake that: • The bulk will correspond with the sample in quality • The buyer will have a reasonable opportunity to compare the bulk with the sample • The goods will be free from defects which would not be apparent from reasonable examination of the sample

2.8 Other sections of the Act deal with the following issues.

- When ownership passes from a seller to a buyer (Sections 16–20)
- The seller's duty to deliver, and the buyer's duty to accept and pay for, goods in various circumstances (Sections 27–31)
- Remedies for breach of contract by the buyer, eg if the seller isn't paid (Sections 41–50)
- Remedies for breach of contract by the seller, eg if goods aren't delivered as contracted (Sections 51–54).

You shouldn't be required to know the detailed provisions at this stage of your studies: you will encounter them when you progress further.

2.9 Similar provisions, in the context of the supply of goods and services, are contained in the *Supply of Goods and Services Act 1982.*

2.10 You should be able to come up with examples for each scenario envisaged by the implied terms covered in Table 8.1. For example, a supermarket might purchase products described as 'biodegradable plastic bags' from a supplier, but subsequently find out that the bags are not biodegradable. An office manager might buy wallpaper based on samples, only to find that the batch of paper delivered is of a slightly different colour – and the supplier hadn't warned that this could happen.

2.11 If an important implied term (called a 'condition') is not met, the buyer is entitled to insist that it *is* met or, more usually, to receive *damages*: monetary compensation for any economic loss resulting from the breach of contract. The purpose of damages is to restore the injured party to the same position he would be in if the contract had been performed. If a seller fails to deliver goods, for example, damages should equal the difference between the agreed contract price and the cost of obtaining the goods elsewhere.

Another relevant statute: the Unfair Contract Terms Act 1977

2.12 The express terms of a contract may attempt to exclude or limit terms implied by statute: a supplier stating, for example, that he accepts no responsibility for goods not conforming to description or sample.

2.13 However, this might unfairly limit the rights of buyers, and is therefore subject to certain restrictions. The *Unfair Contract Terms Act 1977* restricts the exclusion or limitation of liability for:

- Negligence (s 2): that is, the breach of a contract obligation (express or implied) to take reasonable care *or* the breach of the common law duty to take reasonable care.
- Breach of implied terms (s 3). Liability for breach cannot be excluded at all in consumer contracts (to protect consumer interests), and only in other contracts if the exclusion is 'reasonable' and fair, taking into account other factors: whether the buyer was forced by circumstances or inducements to agree to the term, whether the buyer understood (or ought to have understood) the implications of the term and so on.

3 Employment law

Introduction

3.1 Employment law deals with the legal relationship between employers and employees, securing both individual employment rights (such as protection from unfair dismissal or the right to equal pay and opportunity) and collective employment rights (such as the right to trade union membership and consultation). Some aspects of the employment relationship are governed by the *common law* on contracts: principles such as duty of care (in relation to health and safety) and so on. However, this is an area that has been increasingly addressed by *statute law*. Key areas of employment legislation are summarised in Table 8.2.

3.2 We have included the key statutes mainly to highlight (a) the amount of legislation employers have to take into account and (b) the frequency with which legislation changes.

3.3 You might also note a strong relationship between the political environment and the legal environment. Much of the legislation of the 1980s was passed by Conservative governments seeking to remove constraints on business, reducing individual protections and limiting trade union power. Legislation by the subsequent Labour governments has gone the other way, supporting trade union activity and individual rights (the minimum wage; family friendly working hours; minority rights and so on). Meanwhile, the influence of *EC law* has increased steadily.

Table 8.2 *Key UK employment legislation*

FIELD	PURPOSE	KEY STATUTES
Equal opportunity	Outlawing various forms of discrimination	*Race Relations Act 1968* *Sex Discrimination Act 1975/86* *Disability Discrimination Act 2005*
Pay	Providing minimum wages and employee information on pay Providing equal pay for men and women doing 'work of equal value'	*Wages Act 1986* *National Minimum Wage (Enforcement) Act 2003* *Equal Pay Act 1970*
Heath and safety at work	Providing healthy and safe working environments and practices	*Factories Act 1961* *Health & Safety at Work Act 1974*
Employment protection	Protecting employees from unfair dismissal and redundancy	*Employment Protection Act 1975* *Employment Acts (1980s, 2002)* *Employment Rights Act 1996* *Employment Relations Acts 1999/2004*
Industrial relations	Regulating the rights and activities of trade unions and employee representatives	*Industrial Relations Act 1971* *Trade Union and Labour Relations Acts 1974/1976/1992* *Trade Union Reform and Employment Rights Act 1993*
Flexible working	Giving working parents the right to request flexible working arrangements Protecting the rights of fixed-term (short-contract) employees	*Employment Act 2002*

Outsourcing and redundancies

3.4 Most employment protection law should be considered beyond the scope of the syllabus, but the provisions relating to the protection of employee rights in the event of outsourcing is arguably more directly relevant to purchasing.

3.5 The *Transfer of Undertakings (Protection of Employment) Regulations 2006* – known as TUPE – are intended to preserve employees' rights when an undertaking, or part of one, is transferred to a new employer *or* when a 'service provision change' takes place (eg where services are outsourced or re-assigned from one contractor to another).

3.6 The criteria for employees to be protected under the Act are as follows.

- That there is a transfer of economic activity
- That the employees were employed immediately before the transfer
- That they were employed in the activity being transferred and
- That their contracts would have been terminated by the transfer.

3.7 The act protects such employees in various ways.

- Employees employed when the business changes hands automatically become employees of the new employer, with the right to the same terms and conditions as set out in their original contract of employment and any negotiated agreements (unless variations are justified on economic, technical or organisational – ETO – grounds).
- Representatives of any employees affected by the transfer (eg their recognised trade unions) have the right to be informed and consulted about the timing, reasons and implementation of the transfer.

- If employees are dismissed because of the transfer, and the dismissal is deemed justified on ETO grounds, this is defined as redundancy: employees have other rights (eg to notice, redundancy pay and time off to look for other work) under various Employment Protection and Employment Rights Acts.

3.8 The legislation also protects the new employer, by placing a duty on the old employer to provide information about the transferring workforce: this is called 'employee liability information'.

3.9 From Table 8.2, you can see that this is part of a much broader body of employment rights and protection law. Dismissals, redundancies and trade union consultations are complex matters – and beyond the scope and depth of this syllabus. If in doubt, a purchasing officer would in any case consult the HR or legal department of the organisation before taking any action in regard to staff.

4 Equal opportunity

The law on equal opportunity

4.1 'Equal opportunity' in an employment context means that everyone has a fair chance of getting a job, accessing training and benefits and competing for promotion, regardless of individual differences or minority status. It is, effectively, non-discrimination or anti-discrimination.

4.2 UK legislation outlaws discrimination in a number of key areas.

4.3 The **Sex Discrimination Act** prohibited certain types of discrimination in employment against women (and men) by reason of sex, marital status (eg if an employer believes that a single man will be able to devote more time to the job), and change of sex or gender reassignment. The Employment Equality (Sexual Orientation) Regulations 2003 also outlaw discrimination on the grounds of sexual orientation. Special provision was made under the **Equal Pay Act** (and later amendment regulations implementing the European Equal Pay Directive), for women to have the right to claim equal pay and conditions for work of equal value to that of a man in the organisation.

4.4 The **Race Relations Act** covered discrimination on grounds of colour, race, nationality, and ethnic or national origin. The Employment Equality Regulations also prohibit discrimination on the grounds of religion or belief.

4.5 The **Disability Discrimination Act** covered discrimination against disabled persons. In addition, the employer has a duty to make reasonable adjustments to working arrangements or to the physical features of premises where these constitute a disadvantage to a particular disabled employee.

4.6 The **Employment Equality (Age) Regulations** banned discrimination on the basis of age (old or young) in terms of recruitment, promotion, access to training and rights to claim unfair dismissal or receive redundancy payments. It also bans companies from setting compulsory retirement ages below 65 (unless this can be objectively justified), and introduces the right for employees to request working beyond retirement age (which must be considered by employers, although not necessarily granted).

4.7 There are three basic types of unlawful discrimination under the legislation.

- **Direct discrimination** is where one group is treated less favourably than another. Using age as an example, direct discrimination would include not providing medical insurance to employees aged 50 or older.
- **Indirect discrimination** is where an employer applies a provision, criterion or practice to all groups equally, but this has the *effect* of putting one group at a particular disadvantage, without justification. Examples might include: changing shift patterns to include early morning starts, as this would disadvantage women (who are usually responsible for child care).
- **Harassment** is defined as unwanted conduct (verbal or non-verbal) which violates a person's dignity, or creates an intimidating, hostile, degrading, humiliating or offensive environment for a person. Examples include: placing vital objects on a high shelf, where a disabled person cannot reach; derogatory comments about a woman's appearance; or racist jokes.

4.8 Since October 2007, it has been the responsibility of the new Commission for Equality and Human Rights (CEHR) to promote equality and tackle discrimination in the areas of sex, race, disability and age, religion/belief and sexual orientation. (Previously, separate commissions existed in each area.) Most of the legislation relating to discrimination has now been consolidated in the **Equality Act 2010** which strengthens and supersedes many of the Acts described above.

Equal opportunity in practice

4.9 In order to respond to the legislative provisions, organisations may have to pay particular attention to policies and practices for recruitment, selection and employee development. There is always a risk that a disappointed job applicant (or training applicant or promotion prospect) will attribute his lack of success to discrimination – especially if a given ethnic minority, sex or other group is already poorly represented in the organisation (or in management posts), or if policies on equal opportunity are not clear.

4.10 Here are some common compliance issues.

- Job advertising: employers should not imply or state any intention to discriminate, and should not place advertisements where minority groups will be disadvantaged in accessing them. This may rule out recruiting by word-of-mouth, using the existing workforce, for example, if it is not broadly representative.
- Selection interviewing: employers should not ask non-work-related questions of some groups but not others (eg only asking women about plans to start a family)
- Employers should formulate selection tests which are performance-relevant and do not favour particular groups.

4.11 In addition to compliance, some employers have begun to address the underlying problems of equal opportunities, appointing equal opportunities managers to put issues higher on the corporate agenda, and providing awareness training for managers to encourage a 'managing diversity' orientation.

4.12 Flexible policies on working hours and career shapes facilitate employment for women with family responsibilities. Under the Employment Act 2002, mothers and fathers of children under six years of age (or disabled children under 18) have the right to request a flexible working arrangement. Career-break and return-to-work schemes may also be developed, including training for women returners. The provision of workplace childcare facilities is another possibility.

4.13 The accelerated development of women and minority groups can be achieved by 'fast-tracking' school leavers and graduates, and posting managerial vacancies internally, giving more opportunities for movement up the ladder for groups currently at lower levels of the organisation. Positive action may be taken to train disadvantaged groups, or to encourage them to undertake training in which they have previously been under-represented (the one area in which positive discrimination is permissible). The Metropolitan Police in London, for example, piloted a scheme of pre-training training (in literacy, numeracy, current affairs, physical fitness and interpersonal skills) to prepare applicants from minority groups to compete on an equal basis for training places.

4.14 In the area of disability, similar positive action policies may include the provision of wheelchair access, braille or large-print versions of documentation, text-based telecommunications systems and so on. You might like to think what adjustments might be made to facilitate work (and avoid harassment) for members of religious groups in the workplace.

5 Health and safety at work

Statute law on health and safety at work

5.1 In 1972, the Royal Commission on Safety and Health at Work reported that unnecessarily large numbers of days were being lost each year through industrial accidents, injuries and diseases, because of the 'attitudes, capabilities and performance of people and the efficiency of the organisational systems within which they work'. Since then, major legislation has been brought into effect in the UK, most notably:

- The Health and Safety at Work Act 1974
- Various regulations implementing EU directives on health and safety, including:
  — The Manual Handling Operations Regulations 1992
  — The Workplace (Health, Safety and Welfare) Regulations 1992
  — The Provision and Use of Work Equipment Regulations 1992
  — The Health and Safety (Display Screen Equipment) Regulations 1992
  — The Control of Substances Hazardous to Health Regulations 1994
  — The Fire Precautions (Workplace) Regulations 1997
  — The Management of Health and Safety at Work Regulations 1999

5.2 We will not be able to cover their provisions in detail here. Just be aware that the framework for HR policy in the area of health and safety is extensive, detailed – and constantly changing.

Why focus on health and safety?

5.3 Wider attention has been given to health and safety issues, with consumer demand for social responsibility by organisations (underpinned by the competitive need to attract and retain quality labour) and widespread exposure of abuses through disasters such as the Bhopal chemical plant and Piper Alpha oil rig explosions. So why should organisations plan for health and safety at work?

- To protect people from pain and suffering (obviously, we hope)
- To comply with relevant legal and policy standards
- To minimise the costs of accidents and ill-health (including disruption to work, sickness benefits, repairs, replacement staff, legal claims etc)
- To enhance their ability to attract and retain quality staff
- To avoid negative PR and enhance their employer brand and reputation for corporate social responsibility.

The Health and Safety at Work Act 1974

5.4 Under the Health and Safety at Work Act 1974, every employer has a general duty to ensure the health, safety and welfare at work of all employees, so far as is reasonably practicable. Various aspects of this responsibility, included in the Act and subsequent Regulations, are set out in Table 8.3.

Table 8.3 *Employer and employee duties in managing health and safety*

HEALTH AND SAFETY AT WORK ACT 1974	
Employee's duties	**Employer's duties**
• To take reasonable care of himself and others affected by his acts or omissions at work • To cooperate with the employer in carrying out his duties (including enforcing safety rules) • Not to interfere intentionally or recklessly with any machinery or equipment provided in the interests of health and safety	• To provide safe systems (work practices) • To provide a safe and healthy work environment (well-lit, warm, ventilated, hygienic and so on) • To maintain all plant and equipment to a necessary standard of safety • To support safe working practices with information, instruction, training and supervision • To consult with safety representatives appointed by a recognised trade union • To appoint a safety committee to monitor safety policy if asked to do so • To communicate safety policy and measures to all staff, clearly and in writing
THE MANAGEMENT OF HEALTH AND SAFETY AT WORK REGULATIONS 1992	
Employee's duties	**Employer's duties**
• To inform the employer of any situation which may pose a danger	• To carry out risk assessment, generally in writing, of all work hazards, on a continuous basis • To introduce controls to reduce risks • To assess the risks to anyone else affected by their work activities • To share hazard and risk information with other employers, including those on adjoining premises, other site occupiers and all subcontractors entering the premises • To initiate or revise safety policies in the light of the above • To identify employees who are especially at risk (other legislation cites pregnant women, young workers, shift-workers and part-time workers) • To provide fresh and appropriate training in safety matters • To provide information to employees (including temporary workers) about health and safety • To employ competent safety and health advisers.
HEALTH AND SAFETY (CONSULTATION WITH EMPLOYEES) REGULATIONS 1996	
Employee's duties	**Employer's duties**
	• To consult all employees on health and safety matters (such as the planning of health and safety training, changes in equipment or procedures which may substantially affect health and safety at work, or the health and safety consequences of introducing new technology)

8

5.5 Other regulations cover particular safety and health risks in the workplace, and in particular industries: guidelines are available from the Health and Safety Executive. You may also encounter particular measures (eg in relation to manual handling and dangerous substances) in your studies for subjects such as *Purchasing Operations.*

Health and safety in practice

5.6 Apart from obviously dangerous equipment in offices and factories, there are many hazards to be found in the modern working environment, and the prevention of accidents is a major aspect of health and safety policy: advising and warning about safe and unsafe procedures, activities and attitudes.

5.7 The Workplace (Health, Safety and Welfare) Regulations 1992 provide for a range of safety measures. Machinery and equipment should be properly maintained, and fenced if dangerous. Floors, passages and stairs must be properly constructed and maintained. Falls and falling objects should be prevented by erecting effective physical safeguards. Windows, doors and gates should be made of safe materials and fitted with any necessary safety devices. Fire precautions should be taken; appropriate firefighting equipment and clearly marked (and unobstructed) escape routes should be provided. Fire alarms should be installed and regularly tested.

5.8 Various high-risk activities may be the subject of policies and procedures.

- The lifting of heavy objects ('manual handling operations')
- The safe handling, storage and disposal of hazardous chemicals and other substances. Hazards may include poisoning, burning and allergies, as a result of exposure – and also serious conditions (such as cancers and lung diseases) linked to substances such as lead, radioactive materials, asbestos and coal dust.
- The use of computer workstations. Attention may be given to the ergonomic design of workstations (to avoid strain), the control of monitor glare, and user practices (poor posture, insufficient work breaks and so on).

5.9 Many organisations now also have policies relating to personal health and safety: alcohol and drug abuse (affecting work behaviour); non-smoking workplaces; and positive health promotion (eg stress management, health checks, education, fitness programmes and so on).

5.10 Gather some examples from your own organisation's health and safety policies and practices, for use as illustrations in the exam (if required).

6 Other law affecting purchasing

6.1 The syllabus doesn't specifically mention the following areas, but it is worth being aware of them as potential examples of statutory influences on purchasing activity.

Competition law

6.2 Governments generally want to support free competition, as this is arguably in the best interests of consumers and the economy as a whole.

6.3 The Competition Act 1998 is one measure designed to protect competition in the UK.

- Chapter 1 of the Act prohibits agreements and concerted practices (eg cartels and price fixing agreements) which prevent, restrict or distort competition, or are intended to do so, and which may affect trade within the UK. An agreement is unlikely to be considered as having an appreciable effect on the market unless the combined market share of the parties involved is greater than 25%.

- Chapter 2 prohibits abuse by one or more undertakings of a dominant position in a market, which may affect trade within the UK. A 'dominant position' is largely determined by the extent to which the undertaking(s) can act independently of competitors: this would usually mean a market share of more than 40%. 'Abuse' includes conduct such as imposing unfair purchase or selling prices; limiting production or technical development to the detriment of consumers; or applying different trading conditions in such a way as to place certain parties at a competitive disadvantage.

6.4 The Fair Trading Act 1973 also gives wide powers to the Office of Fair Trading to investigate and regulate monopolies and mergers, while the Enterprise Act 2002 makes it a criminal offence to operate a price cartel.

6.5 Similar measures, in regard to competition within the EU, are provided by the Treaty of Rome Articles 81 (anti-competitive agreements) and 82 (abuse of a monopoly position).

Public sector procurement

6.6 The *Public Contracts Regulations 2006* apply to public authorities and utilities for purchases above a given financial threshold. The purposes of the regulations, and the **EU public procurement directives** on which they were based, are: to open up the choice of potential suppliers to public sector bodies, reducing costs through competition; to open up new, non-discriminatory and genuinely competitive markets for suppliers; to facilitate the free movement of goods and services within the EU; and to ensure that public sector bodies award contracts efficiently and without discrimination.

6.7 The regulations set out rules for the following areas.

- The open advertising of tenders through the EU
- Contract award procedures and time limits for the issuing and receipt of tenders
- Award criteria. In general, buyers are obliged to award the contract on the basis of the lowest quoted price, or on the basis of the 'economically most advantageous' tender (in which case they must explain by what non-price criteria they mean to assess 'economic advantage'). This is designed to ensure that criteria are clearly defined, non-discriminatory – and not leaving room for manipulative post-tender negotiation.
- Suppliers' right to feedback: unsuccessful bidders have the right to a debrief, at their request, in order to understand why they did not win the contract.

6.8 You will study these requirements in detail later in your CIPS studies.

The key point being...

6.9 Of course, there are many other relevant areas, such as corporate governance, fraud prevention, protection of intellectual property (copyrights and patents), data protection and freedom of information. But we have to stop somewhere! The key point is: purchasing professionals really need to monitor the legal environment...

Chapter summary

- The legal environment consists of statute law (Acts of Parliament and other statutory instruments); European Community law; and case law, including principles of common law and equity determined as a result of legal precedent.
- Contract law is concerned with legally binding agreements between two or more parties. The Sale of Goods Act 1979 draws together the legal principles relating to contracts, including implied terms as to title, sale by description, satisfactory quality and fitness for purpose, and sale by sample.
- Employment law deals with the legal relationship between employers and employees, both individually and collectively. Legislation in this area covers issues such as employment protection (including TUPE transfers).
- Equal opportunity law is designed to outlaw discrimination in areas such as sex and sexual orientation, race, disabilities, age and religion.
- Legislation on health and safety at work is designed to ensure that employees are protected as far as possible from accidents and ill health arising from the working environment. Duties are imposed on both employers and employees to achieve this.
- Other areas of legislation relevant to purchasers include: competition law; and the particular regulations applying to purchasing in the public sector.

Self-test questions

Numbers in brackets refer to paragraphs where you can check your answers

1   Explain the importance of the legal environment. (1.2)

2   List the sources of English law. (1.3)

3   What are the four essential elements of a contract? (2.2)

4   What implied terms are provided by sections 12–15 of the Sale of Goods Act 1979? (2.7)

5   What remedies are available to a buyer if an important implied term of a sales contract is not met? (2.11)

6   When do the TUPE Regulations 2006 apply, and what are an employer's duties under the Regulations? (3.5–3.7)

7   In what areas is discrimination outlawed under UK equal opportunities legislation? (4.3–4.6)

8   What are an employee's duties under the Health and Safety at Work Act? (Table 8.3)

9   Identify three potential causes of accidents in the workplace, and suggest what might be done to minimise the risk. (5.7, 5.8)

10   What are the purposes of the EU public sector procurement directives? (6.6)

CHAPTER 9

Environmental Factors

Assessment criteria and indicative content

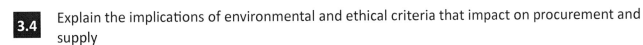

3.4 Explain the implications of environmental and ethical criteria that impact on procurement and supply

- Environmental criteria such as natural risks, waste emissions, pollution and energy efficiency that impact on organisations

Section headings

1 The natural environment
2 Current environmental concerns
3 Pressure for environmental responsibility
4 Environmental policy
5 The contribution of purchasing to 'green' business

Introduction

In this chapter, we cover factors relating to the natural environment.

Note that when you read or use the phrase 'environmental factors', you need to be clear whether it refers specifically to the natural environment or 'green' factors (in the sense in which people are concerned about 'the environment') – or whether it is referring to the business or purchasing environment as a whole.

This is a highly fashionable topic at the moment, and a high governmental and organisational priority – for reasons both of sustainability (a stewardship duty to maintain a viable environment for future generations) and of marketing (given increasing stakeholder pressure for nations and organisations to demonstrate responsibility).

We start this chapter with a brief overview of the natural environment, before exploring in more depth some of the key issues and trends which are currently of concern: for example, pollution control and global warming.

We go on to outline the legislation, regulation and international agreements aimed at securing environmental protection, including the Kyoto agreement.

Finally, we explore the processes whereby a business may develop and pursue an environmental policy – and some of the issues that may arise as it does so.

1 The natural environment

Factors in the natural environment

1.1 This aspect of the purchasing environment may be called the 'ecological' environment (ecology being the study of organisms in their natural environment); the 'natural' environment (ie relating to nature); or the 'natural resource' environment (since the organisation draws resources from nature). 'The environment' has become a kind of popular shorthand for nature and 'green issues'.

1.2 Here are some factors in the natural environment which are relevant to purchasing.

- The weather – and more generally, climate factors. These may affect commodity prices, supply and logistics: for example, drought and flood affecting agricultural production, or the risk of hurricanes disrupting shipping and road transport. Weather effects, in particular, cannot be reliably forecast, and represent a significant supply risk.
- Natural resources, such as oil, coal and other minerals, and farmed or gathered materials and ingredients used in products, such as cotton, wool and foodstuffs. The availability, quality and price of such supplies will be of key interest to buyers.
- The impact of business on the natural environment, in terms of land use, pollution and so on.
- Specific issues of environmental concern, such as deforestation (particularly the loss of rainforests), the reduction of world fish stocks through overfishing, the loss of biodiversity, or climate change ('global warming'). We will discuss a number of the 'hot' eco-issues further on in the chapter.
- Governmental, pressure group and public concern, and pressure applied on organisations, in any or all of the above areas. Some are the subject of international agreements and targets (eg Kyoto). Others are the subject of legislation (eg on electronic and electrical waste, and lead emissions by cars). Some are the subject of incentives (eg 'polluter pays' taxes and consumer 'green brand' awards), while others are subject only to public awareness and consumer pressure for social responsibility.

Local, national and global issues

1.3 Some issues may be local in their scope and effects: for example, a factory discharging effluent into a local river; the risk of local flooding; or local traffic congestion and pollution (noise, dirt, vibration and air pollution) caused by transportation.

1.4 Some issues are national in their impact (for example, in the UK, national resource issues such as water or energy consumption, deforestation and the loss of arable land to urbanisation) and in their management (for example, UK legislation such as the Clean Air Act, and public sector sustainability targets). Other countries will have a different set of problems: drought, water management and salination (increasing salt concentration in water and soil) in Australia, say, or deforestation in Asia and South America, because of logging and/or demand for land to be cleared for agriculture. You should identify the key environmental issues affecting your own country.

1.5 Some issues are international in their scope and management. Increasingly, the world faces genuinely 'global' problems, such as climate change, resource depletion or damage to the ozone layer. Although it has been slow happening, there are now also concerted international responses to environmental issues: for example, EU directives, the Kyoto Agreement on climate change, and OECD recommendations.

1.6 To get a flavour of these different levels of concern, you might like to check out the environmental policy statements of:

- Your local government body
- The UK Environment Agency
- The European Environment Agency

1.7 You might also browse the websites of international environmental pressure groups such as Greenpeace or the David Suzuki Foundation – and any commercial organisations you are interested in.

Impact on purchasing

1.8 The kinds of factors outlined above may influence purchasing activity in various ways.

1.9 Increasing consumer concern will place pressure on organisations to adapt their products and processes to be more environment-friendly, because consumers will prefer 'green' brands (such as The Body Shop) – and may boycott brands with a poor environmental reputation (such as BP following an oil spill). Purchasing will have a key role in 'greening' products and processes, as we will see later: it will also be affected by a rise or fall in demand due to green consumption.

1.10 Government policy and legislation creates compliance issues. The UK Waste Electrical and Electronic Equipment (WEEE) Regulations 2006, for example, follow an EU Directive which makes manufacturers, sellers of branded products, importers (including purchasers) and exporters of electronic and electrical products responsible for the costs of their collection, treatment, disposal and recycling.

1.11 There may be financial penalties for poor environmental performance (eg fines for non-compliance or 'polluter pays' taxes). On the other hand, there may also be a cost in implementing a corporate environmental policy (eg more expensive materials, recycling processes, tighter controls and general change management) – and in implementing a national policy (eg the Climate Change Levy used to fund the Carbon Trust).

1.12 Costs of obtaining natural resources and commodities may rise as supplies fall, whether because of long-term factors (such as depletion), or short-term supply factors (eg weather affecting agricultural production, or political unrest disrupting gas supplies from Russia, say).

1.13 Cost savings may be achievable by a firm, for example by reducing its energy consumption, reducing its product packaging or using recycled materials.

1.14 Natural events (eg severe weather or earthquake) pose a risk for supply, potentially disrupting production or transport infrastructure. Purchasers may need to secure 'back-up' sources of supply and purchase insurances to cover the risk. They may also choose to support the supply chain: when a 2007 earthquake in Tokyo forced one of Toyota's key component suppliers to halt production, for example, Toyota provided 200 staff to help the supplier with its recovery.

9

2 Current environmental concerns

Resource depletion and management

2.1 The factors in the natural environment which are currently known about, and of concern, are many and various. Start collecting a dossier of examples of 'green' issues that interest you, and what corporations are (or are not) doing about them: they will give you a stock of useful illustrations for an exam answer. We will just look at some key issues, briefly, here.

2.2 A number of issues are of current concern, in regard to resource depletion and management.

- There is an increasing depletion of non-renewable resources: resources which cannot be replenished once supply is exhausted. Key examples include oil, coal and other minerals, agricultural land and rainforests (given the long time-scale for regeneration of such complex eco-systems). There is increasing pressure on businesses (and society in general) to limit or minimise the use of non-renewable resources, in order to support sustainability.
- There is also a challenge in keeping renewable resources productive. The world is unlikely to 'run out' of resources such as soil, water, fish stocks and clean air – but the quality and productivity of those resources is being reduced by overuse, pollution and other forms of environmental damage. The yield of agricultural land, for example, is significantly reduced by overuse, erosion, salination, irrigation difficulties, pollution and other effects.
- Both the above factors create a challenge of finding new resources: for example, vegetable-based fuels or bio-fuels, and renewable energy sources such as water, wind and solar power. The UK has recently set a target of 10% of its electricity coming from renewable sources, for example, and Virgin Airlines – among other private sector firms – are investing heavily in research on bio-fuels, to offset their impact on the environment through the use of non-renewable (and pollutant) fuels.

2.3 A related area of concern is the increasing rate of species extinction and the loss of **biodiversity** through the destruction of natural habitats which support varied ecosystems and plant and animal species. This may represent a depletion of resources (eg plants with medicinal properties as yet unresearched), but also represents issues of social cost and legacy: the desire not to leave future generations with an impoverished biosphere and environmental problems.

2.4 CIPS defines biodiversity as 'the total variety of life on Earth'. Its *Corporate Social Responsibility* guidelines argue that: 'In principle, most people support the idea of preserving diversity of habitats, genetic profiles and species. It is a responsibility of organisations to minimise any adverse impact on these areas'.

Environmental damage

2.5 It has been recognised, ever since the early days of the Industrial Revolution, that industrialisation has an impact on the natural environment. Again, this may take many forms, depending on the location and nature of industrial activity.

2.6 There is a steady loss of arable land available for food production, due to industrial and urban development, putting pressure on food supply chains and prices.

2.7 There has also been destruction of rainforest land on a massive scale, both for forestry (for wood and paper industry products) and to clear more arable land to support the development of rainforest communities. This damages the environment on several levels.

- Rainforests are complex eco-systems which house a high proportion of the world's plants, insects and other unique species: the destruction of habitats causes a drastic loss of biodiversity
- Rainforests are some of the few remaining large-scale forested areas. Trees and other plants are a key mechanism in maintenance and 'cleaning' of the earth's atmosphere, taking in carbon dioxide and generating oxygen. The destruction of forests therefore contributes to a build up of carbon dioxide in the atmosphere, making it both less breathable and more prone to global warming (as discussed below).
- Rainforests contain unique plant species, which have been used for their medicinal properties by indigenous communities. Their destruction represents a loss of potential – as yet unresearched – resources.
- Rainforests are also the habitat of small indigenous groups, whose culture and way of life is threatened by the encroachment of industrialised society.

2.8   Another range of issues surrounds various forms of industrial pollution and their effects. Examples include air pollution, through vehicle and factory emissions, dust and chemical sprays; soil pollution, through the seepage or burial of industrial waste, or the use of chemical fertilisers; the contamination of wetlands, rivers and oceans, through the seepage or discharge of effluent (liquid waste), or accidental oil and chemical spillages; and noise pollution, through machine and vehicle noise.

2.9   The discharge and disposal of waste products, particularly in terms of non-biodegradable, toxic and radioactive materials, is the subject of legislation in many countries, with regulations on safe handling, transport and disposal. This has created pressure for the development of recyclable products and materials, and for producers to take responsibility for the collection and disposal of potentially damaging waste products (such as obsolete electrical and electronic goods).

2.10   You might think of further examples from the news media or your own experience: the scarring of areas of natural beauty for mining; the loss of bird and animal species as natural habitats are taken over for housing or transport infrastructure; and so on.

2.11   Local authorities and firms increasingly have policies about waste reduction, recycling, land reclamation or re-beautification, safe waste disposal, pollution and emissions control, the preservation of 'green corridors' and habitats, and so on. In addition, businesses are implementing policies such as the following.

- Reducing product packaging, or using sustainable raw materials in packaging (eg recycled paper)
- Seeking to use sustainable raw materials (eg not using rainforest wood and paper products, using recycled materials where possible)
- Discouraging plastic carrier bag usage by shoppers (in retail environments)
- Developing recyclable materials and products, and encouraging recycling via reverse logistics provisions
- Setting targets to reduce waste products and/or to reduce the amount of waste sent to landfill (as opposed to re-use or recycling)
- Eliminating the use of chemicals and pesticides (in food production, say)
- Reducing transport emissions through 'green' vehicles and route planning

9

Climate change

2.12 Climate change or 'global warming' is perhaps the 'hottest' topic in environmental politics (no pun intended!), with a number of major research reports and a major film *(Al Gore's An Inconvenient Truth)* raising the profile of the issue for governments and pressure groups worldwide.

2.13 The science of climate change is still under debate, with some scientists claiming that the causes of atmospheric temperature fluctuations are not clear, or that such fluctuations occurred naturally long before human (let alone industrial) intervention in the environment. However, there is fairly widespread political consensus on the prevailing theory.

2.14 Essentially, 'greenhouse gases' in the atmosphere, including carbon dioxide, fulfil an essential function in keeping the earth warm. Excess levels of these gases, however, can raise the temperature too far, causing the melting of polar ice-caps, the rising of sea levels and changes to global climate patterns. Greenhouse gases are produced by natural as well as industrial processes, but current levels in the atmosphere appear to be higher than in pre-industrialisation eras, and have been attributed to factors such as transportation and energy use.

2.15 Global warming and climate change may have a range of severe consequences, including the flooding of coastal areas and the displacement of communities; the disruption of agriculture and food production; and the increase in severe weather events such as hurricanes and droughts (which – among other ill effects – may disrupt supply).

2.16 In order to counter the threat, societies and corporations are urged to reduce greenhouse gas emissions, and to reduce their 'carbon footprint': that is, the total impact of their activities on the amount of carbon dioxide (CO_2) in the atmosphere. Emissions-reducing projects include renewable and 'clean' energy (such as wind farms or hydro-electric plants), energy efficiency projects and re-forestation projects.

2.17 Here are some practical measures that can be taken by individual firms.

- Setting policies and targets for reducing carbon emissions (and ideally becoming carbon neutral) and monitoring carbon footprint
- Minimising the use of non-renewable (fossil fuel) energy in all activities, and sourcing or generating 'green' (renewable) electricity
- Reducing business travel and the air freight of goods (and/or labelling air-freighted products to give consumers the choice); planning road haulage to minimise fuel use and emissions; moving towards the use of bio-diesel in lorry fleets; and using 'green' company car fleets
- Carbon offsetting (ideally, where no other method of reducing CO_2 emissions is available). Individuals, companies or governments can purchase financial instruments called 'carbon offsets' (representing the fruits of emissions-reducing projects) to compensate for their own greenhouse gas emissions. (The Kyoto Protocol sanctioned offsets as a way for governments and private companies to earn 'carbon credits' which can be traded in a compliance market.)
- Carbon labelling: supporting the work of the Carbon Trust to develop the labelling of consumer products and services with their carbon impact
- Developing and selling products with a lower carbon impact (eg low-energy use household appliances, non-HFC-gas refrigerators and air-conditioning systems, clothes which can be washed at lower temperatures)
- Mobilising and supporting key suppliers and logistics providers in reducing their carbon

emissions, and making this a criterion for supplier selection and evaluation.

- Mobilising and supporting customers in reducing their carbon emissions. Marks & Spencer, for example, are now educating their customers on carbon footprint reduction (in a joint campaign with the World Wildlife Fund, WWF), supporting the carbon labelling of their products, and siting retail outlets to encourage the use of public transport and cycling (to reduce car usage).

2.18 The **Kyoto Protocol** is a proposal of the international Framework Convention on Climate Change, aiming to reduce greenhouse gases – and therefore to prevent human-driven climate change. The protocol came into effect in 2005, and now has over 180 signatories: a significant achievement in securing global co-operation. It requires signatories to commit to targets for reducing national CO2 emissions: the UK has adopted the target of cutting national carbon dioxide emissions by 20% by 2010, for example.

2.19 The protocol also established the 'Clean Development Mechanism' (CDM), which validates and measures emissions-reduction projects (renewable energy production, changes in land use, re-forestation and so on). This allows entities that have difficulty meeting their emissions quotas to offset, by buying CDM-approved Certified Emissions Reductions.

2.20 The USA is the only developed country not to ratify the Kyoto treaty, but debate continues to rage about the usefulness of the protocol and the impact of reducing emissions on national economies and employment.

3 Pressure for environmental responsibility

Environmental law and regulation

3.1 The impetus for firms to become environmentally responsible may come from a number of sources.

3.2 Some areas may be specifically covered by legislation and regulations. For example, the EU has a set of Emissions Standards for all new road vehicles, trains, barges and 'non-road mobile machinery' (such as tractors). Other EU directives include a wide range of areas such as: the disposal of waste electrical and electronic products; the control of landfill use and waste incineration; the protection of water quality, freshwater fish, and bathing waters; the control of agricultural chemicals; the reduction or elimination of pollution; the protection of habitats; the control of the discharge of dangerous substances; and the safe disposal of batteries.

3.3 The Environment Agency in the UK has the responsibility of regulating business and industry: implementing EU directives nationally, issuing permits, monitoring compliance and carrying out risk assessments. There are five basic approaches to regulation.

- Direct regulation: enforcing legislation, and issuing permits, which typically set limits to control pollution levels, and require operators to carry out management processes.
- Environmental (or 'polluter pays') taxes, such as the Landfill Tax or Climate Change Levy.
- Offset or trading schemes, such as the EU Emissions Trading Scheme (for greenhouse gases) and the Landfill Allowances Trading Scheme. Participants can choose either to operate within their allowance (eg by reducing emissions or resource use), *or* buy extra allowances in the market to offset any excess: they can also sell surplus allowances if they perform better than expected.

- Voluntary or negotiated agreements, jointly agreed by businesses (usually to avoid the threat of legislation or compulsory regulation). The motor industry, for example, has a voluntary agreement with the EU on emission reduction targets, and other agreements are in force in the chemical industry and agricultural sector (on the use of pesticides). The Environment Agency monitors compliance.
- Education and advice: the promotion of regulatory requirements, risk assessment consultancy, and showcasing emerging issues and successful initiatives.

Pressure groups and green consumerism

3.4 In addition, you should be aware of the wide range of pressure groups which promote environmental causes and issues; protest (and encourage consumer action) against poor environmental performers; and/or showcase and reward good environmental performers (eg with 'Green Brand' awards, endorsements and collaborative campaigns). You might like to do your own research into one or two such pressure groups which interest you: the Wetlands Trust, Greenpeace, WWF and so on.

3.5 You might also like to browse websites which help consumers to locate 'green' products and brands.

3.6 One of the strongest pressures on corporations to be environmentally responsible has been the rise in green consumerism: the willingness of consumers to choose products, brands and providers on the basis of environmental responsibility. Consumers are increasingly well informed about the environmental performance of firms, and the environmental impact of products (including their energy use, recyclability and carbon footprint), through the internet and the activity of green consumer groups.

3.7 Organisations have faced major consumer boycotts as a result of poor environmental performance. Shell Oil, for example, has been called to account for alleged pollution of waterways in Nigeria; McDonald's for its excess packaging; and cosmetic and pharmaceutical companies for animal testing of products.

3.8 Conversely, organisations such as The Body Shop – and, more recently, Marks & Spencer – have created a strong brand identity and customer loyalty through environmental leadership.

4   Environmental policy

Establishing an environmental policy

4.1 Pressures such as those discussed above have led many organisations to take direct action on environmental responsibility.

4.2 The first step for a firm wishing to establish an environmental policy will be to determine its objectives. This may not be easy: it is not always clear whether Product X is more or less friendly to the environment than Product Y – particularly since the science (eg in the case of climate change) is still being debated. A systematic effort must be made to assemble information from the widest possible range of sources – although, again, it must be remembered that pressure groups may not be the best source of *unbiased* information and views… Research data is now being widely disseminated via Environment Agencies, and some helpful tools have been developed.

4.3 The support of senior management will be essential if any environmental policy is to succeed. If there is no overall corporate policy on environmental issues, the purchasing function may find it difficult to gain stakeholder 'buy in' to the proposal. On the other hand, senior managers may be glad to have change champions in this area, leading the way – and making them look good.

4.4 The next step will be to lay down guidelines on measures that can be instituted within the organisation, usually by negotiation with other functions. For example, purchasing may see the need to minimise packaging, but this may conflict with the ideas of marketing staff.

4.5 Once an organisation takes an environmental stand, it is likely that such attitudes will begin to spread along its supply chain. A 'green' buyer will demand similar commitments from its suppliers, who in turn will pass on the philosophy to second-tier suppliers. A momentum towards better environmental standards is then underway. Of course, this reasoning does not begin – or end – in the purchasing department. On the contrary, it is often an overall corporate policy that leads to change and development. Even so, purchasing staff have an important role to play in giving effect to environmental objectives.

4.6 Ideally, an organisation's environmental policy may also spread along the supply chain in the downstream direction as well – towards consumers – so that they are educated to require green products.

Example: M & S's Plan A

4.7 Here is an example of such a policy in action. In 2007, Marks & Spencer (the UK supermarket chain) launched a new CSR programme called 'Plan A' (so called because 'There is no Plan B'), built on five 'pillars', three of which are environmental.

- *Climate change:* 'We'll aim to make all our UK & Irish operations carbon neutral by 2012. We'll maximise our use of renewable energy and only use offsetting as a last resort. And we'll be helping our customers and suppliers to cut their carbon emissions too.'
- *Waste:* 'We'll significantly reduce the amount of packaging and carrier bags that we use, and find new ways to recycle materials. By 2012, we aim to ensure that none of our clothing or packaging needs to end up as landfill.'
- *Sustainable raw materials:* 'From fish to forests, our goal is to make sure our key raw materials come from the most sustainable sources available to us, protecting the environment and the world's natural resources for future generations.'

4.8 Each of these objectives is broken down into practical action steps (100 in all), involving M & S's own practices; mobilising and supporting suppliers to adopt green practices; and educating and supporting customers to do the same (eg with 'pledges' of participation).

4.9 This is regarded as a cutting edge example of an eco and ethics plan. If you want to know more, the outline of the plan (and progress reports) makes accessible reading: check out http://plana. marksandspencer.com.

Benefits of having a strong environmental policy

4.10 Why should an organisation go to the trouble and cost of developing and implementing an environmental policy?

- A proactive and voluntary display of environmental responsibility may help to stave off more demanding and intrusive legislative requirements and regulation.

- Strong environmental policy goals give the organisation clarity and unity of direction for controls, performance measurement and improvement in this area.
- Strong environmental policy goals give guidance to supply chain partners and customers, gaining their support and compliance.
- A reputation for environmental responsibility may build an attractive brand which will be supported by green consumers; a point of differentiation from competitors for competitive advantage; and a source of customer loyalty.
- A reputation for environmental responsibility may also enhance the organisation's attractiveness as an employer (employer brand) and/or as a customer (for suppliers who are equally committed to green values) and/or as a promotional partner for influential pressure groups (whose members may support the organisation's products).
- Poor environmental performance, and lack of a policy for improvement, may subject the organisation to pressure group opposition, consumer boycott, penalties for non-compliance with legislation and regulation, or environmental (eg polluter pays) taxes.
- Environmental responsibility may be an issue of sustainability: maintaining the resources and markets the organisation itself will require to keep doing business in the future. Squandering resources and alienating communities is counterproductive: 'shooting oneself in the foot'.

5 The contribution of purchasing to 'green' business

5.1 Areas of environmental concern in which purchasing staff have a role to play are summarised by Saunders (*Strategic Purchasing & Supply Chain Management):* Table 9.1.

Table 9.1 *Environmental concerns relevant to purchasing staff*

• Recycling and reusing of materials and waste products (which may require new reverse logistics processes to recover products from consumers)
• Safe disposal of waste products that cannot be recycled
• Supplier selection policies (and tender criteria) to support firms that conform to environmental standards eg with regard to air, water and noise pollution
• Supplier and product selection policies that reflect concern for conservation and renewal of resources
• Safe and animal-friendly testing of products and materials
• Concern for noise, spray, dirt, vibration and congestion in the planning and operation of transportation

5.2 We might also add the following points.

- Acting as the interface between suppliers and product development and design departments, to encourage knowledge-sharing, research and innovation for 'greener' product specifications and collaborative processes
- Gathering and presenting information to demonstrate long-term cost reduction, risk management and sustainability benefits of green policies, in order to secure stakeholder buy-in
- Monitoring, managing and perhaps supporting the environmental performance of suppliers on an ongoing basis, to ensure their compliance with the buyer's environmental standards (in order to minimise the reputational risk of being associated with an environmental disaster)
- Sourcing materials and services for environmental protection and reclamation (eg re-planting trees or cleaning up polluted areas).

5.3 A commitment to avoid buying materials that are harmful to the environment, if alternative products are available at a similar price and quality, should not be controversial. However, *cost* has been a significant obstacle in the past: 'green' products have typically been more expensive than their 'non-green' equivalents. The last few years have seen radical changes in this situation, and in many cases actual savings are to be made in choosing a green or sustainable alternative. (Energy efficient light-bulbs, for example, may cost more upfront but the savings will come further down the line in reduced energy use.)

5.4   If no cost-effective or value-adding green alternatives are available, the buyer may need to work with suppliers to reduce the damaging environmental impact of a product – or with production colleagues to see if the product can be replaced.

5.5   As you will note from our comments above, co-operation with suppliers is an important feature of green procurement. This fits in neatly with modern ideas on supply chain relationships.

5.6   Finally, a timely reminder: human beings are also part of the natural environment! It is comparatively easy to identify and avoid buying products which are dangerous in themselves. It may be less easy to identify harmless products that are, nevertheless, manufactured using processes which place workers in danger, or dangerous to dispose of, or dangerous if stored or used incorrectly by consumers. Attention will have to be given to the whole lifecycle of the product.

9

Chapter summary

- Factors in the natural environment can have an important impact on purchasers: the weather; availability of natural resources; the impact of commercial operations on the natural environment; specific issues of concern, such as deforestation and pollution.
- The natural environment includes factors such as: resource depletion and management; preservation of biodiversity; minimisation of environmental damage (pollution, erosion, waste, deforestation etc); the supply risks posed by weather; climate change – and the influence of legislation, international agreements (such as Kyoto), government policy, pressure groups and public concern on any or all of these issues.
- Increasingly, organisations have faced pressure to exhibit environmental responsibility. This pressure has come from legislation and regulation, the activities of dedicated pressure groups, and the growing concern for environmental issues among consumers.
- The result of this, for many organisations, has been the development of specific environmental policies. There are clear commercial advantages in this process, but such policies are unlikely to succeed unless they are supported by commitment from top management.
- Purchasing can contribute to 'green' operations in a number of areas of materials specification, supplier selection and management, and advocating and justifying change.

Self-test questions

Numbers in brackets refer to paragraphs where you can check your answers

1   List three major factors in the natural environment. (1.2)

2   Give one example each of a local, national and international environmental issue. (1.3–1.5)

3   What can purchasing do to minimise supply risk due to weather? (1.14)

4   Explain the importance of (a) 'biodiversity' and (b) rainforests. (2.3, 2.7)

5   List three ways in which industrial activity may damage the environment. (2.6–2.10)

6   Give three examples of measures to reduce a company's carbon footprint. (2.17)

7   Explain the purpose and achievements of the Kyoto Protocol. (2.18–2.20)

8   Identify five approaches to environmental regulation. (3.3)

9   Explain the benefits of having a strong environmental policy. (4.10)

10 List ways in which purchasing can contribute to environment-friendly operations. (5.1, 5.2)

CHAPTER 10

Social and Ethical Factors

Assessment criteria and indicative content

3.4 Explain the implications of environmental and ethical criteria that impact on procurement and supply

- Ethical and social criteria such as employment rights, community benefits, working conditions and standards that impact on organisations

3.5 Explain the implications of social criteria that impact on procurement and supply

- Changing societal preferences, tastes and fashions, demographics, labour and fair-trade standards and how these can impact on organisations

Section headings

1. The socio-cultural environment
2. Cultural factors
3. Demographic and socio-economic factors
4. Corporate social responsibility and ethics
5. Socio-cultural factors in international supply chains

Introduction

In this chapter, we explore socio-cultural factors and ethical factors. These are broadly 'people' factors, and, more specifically, factors arising from the values and behaviours of people in *groups*: societies, organisations, ethnic groups and so on.

We start the chapter with our usual overview of the impact of socio-cultural factors on purchasing.

We go on to examine what we might call 'local' aspects of culture (that is, the factors within a particular national or organisational culture which influence its members' behaviour) – as opposed to 'international' aspects of culture (the ways in which *differences* in culture can impact on businesses dealing with international stakeholders).

We look at how culture manifests itself in a society or organisation, and at some of the key statistical factors in a population (known as 'demographics') which impact on purchasing. We then go on to include the 'extra E' of the STEEPLE model – ethical factors – as one of the ways in which organisations respond to the social environment.

Finally, we look at the particular socio-cultural challenges of international and cross-cultural business dealings.

1 The socio-cultural environment

1.1 Organisations operate within society, are made up of members of society – and do business (as buyers and sellers) with other organisations and markets of which the same can be said. Society cannot fail to influence business activity.

1.2 Factors in the socio-cultural environment include a wide range of 'people' factors.

- **Demographics**: population size, structure (eg breakdown by age or ethnic group), distribution, movements and characteristics (eg education and employment)
- **Socio-economics**: measures of social class, status, income and wealth, and their impact on consumer spending
- **Social infrastructure**: structural support for education, communications, travel and other activities
- **Culture**: 'the collective programming of the mind which distinguishes the members of one category of people from another' (Hofstede). Culture is the shared assumptions, beliefs, values, behavioural norms, symbols, rituals, stories and artefacts that make our society (or ethnic group, or organisation) distinctively 'us' – or as one writer put it, 'How we do things round here'.
- **Ethics**: the moral values which a society (or organisation) adopts as a guide to defining right and wrong conduct
- **Consumer trends and fashions**: eg patterns of consumer preference, 'hot' products and 'hot' issues which have become or will become important for a society
- **Human resource management** (HRM): attitudes and policies about how people should be employed and managed in organisations.

1.3 These kinds of factors may impact on purchasing in a number of ways.

- A wide range of factors will influence the attitudes and purchasing behaviour of consumers, determining – and potentially changing – the level of demand (and hence supply volume) or the type of goods and services demanded (and hence supply requirements). You might like to run through the list of factors given above and think how each might affect demand for an organisation's goods and services.
- Demographic factors may affect the availability of skilled labour resources, both in purchasing and in the organisation as a whole (so that purchasing may have to contribute to solutions such as outsourcing or subcontracting).
- Cultural factors will influence the attitudes and behaviour of suppliers, affecting the way purchasers are able to negotiate, establish rapport and generally do business with them.
- Cultural, HRM and ethical factors will influence the attitudes and behaviour of purchasing staff, affecting how they can be motivated and managed – and of other members of the organisation, affecting how they perceive and work with the purchasing function.
- *Changes* in socio-cultural factors may require a purchasing response. (A new generation of ICT users, for example, may create pressure to adopt electronic purchasing. The trend towards outsourcing may give purchasing a new role in subcontractor management.)
- *Differences* in socio-cultural factors pose particular challenges for purchasers working with suppliers or colleagues in other countries, or from different backgrounds. This may be a significant barrier to international sourcing (eg different languages, business customs, negotiating styles and regulations). It may also hamper effective communication and collaboration within a multi-cultural purchasing team.

1.4 We will look at some of the key social factors in a little more detail.

2 Cultural factors

Elements of culture

2.1 Culture is the shared ways of behaving and understanding that are distinctive to a particular group of people. This group may be a nation or ethnic group, a social class, a profession or occupation, a gender, or an organisation: each may have its distinctive way of thinking and doing things. These are sometimes called 'spheres' of culture.

2.2 An influential writer on culture, Fons Trompenaars, suggested that culture operates on three levels: Figure 10.1. You might like to picture our pyramid as an 'iceberg', of which only the top third appears above the surface.

Figure 10.1 *Elements of culture*

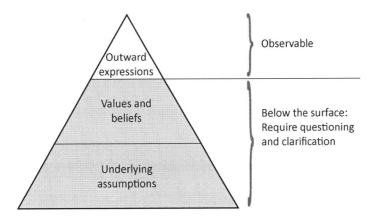

2.3 The most easily recognisable elements of culture, because they are directly observable, are its outward expressions: the part of the iceberg above the water. These elements include behaviour, artefacts and rituals.

- **Behaviour** includes accepted norms of personal and interpersonal conduct (eg negotiation and communication styles); customs and rules defining the right or wrong behaviour in a given situation; fashions and fads; and so on.
- **Artefacts** are products of the culture such as its arts and technology, its myths and heroes, its language and symbols.
- **Rituals**: patterns of behaviour which have symbolic or traditional value, such as social formalities, ceremonies and rites of passage.

2.4 Beneath these outward expressions are the **values and beliefs** which give them their special meaning and significance within the culture. They may be explicit in sayings or mottos, but are often not directly expressed so much as reflected in behaviour, artefacts and rituals. So, for example, a society that believes that age deserves respect will develop behaviours honouring older people, rewarding seniority in organisations, adopting wise elders as role models and so on.

2.5 Beneath values and beliefs lie assumptions: ideas which shape the culture's ways of thinking and behaving – but which have become so ingrained that they are no longer consciously recognised or questioned. The rights of the individual, or the legitimacy of authority, may come into this category, for example.

10

2.6 The 'underlying' elements of culture – like the part of the iceberg that lies under the water – are the ones that often cause problems. They are difficult to manage, whether in societies or organisations, because of the potential for misunderstanding (and, from there, conflict). An important skill of cross-cultural management and purchasing, as we will see, is being aware that, when dealing with other cultures, we don't always know what it is that we don't know. At times, remarks made in conciliatory fashion can cause offence.

2.7 Different countries and cultural sub-groups (different social classes, ethnic backgrounds, religious groups, age groups and so on) may have significantly different norms, values and assumptions, which influence how they do business and manage people, and how consumers develop product and service preferences and buying patterns. An organisation will have to adapt its products, services and processes to the needs of the culture in which it operates.

Organisation culture

2.8 Organisation culture has been defined as 'a pattern of beliefs and expectations shared by an organisation's members, which produce norms that powerfully shape the behaviour of individuals and groups in the organisation' (Schwartz & Davies). It has been summed up as 'the way we do things around here'.

2.9 You should be able to think of examples of each of Trompenaars' elements or manifestations of culture, as they might apply within a work organisation (perhaps using your own organisation as an example).

- Behaviours, for example, might include whether people are familiar or formal with colleagues; the rules of behaviour formulated as part of the disciplinary or ethical code; standard procedures and channels of communication; the 'short-cuts' developed over time in departments; and so on.
- Artefacts may include dress codes, office décor, symbols (such as corporate logos), corporate marketing literature – and indeed all work outputs. Things such as office size may take on a symbolic value, reflecting status or power.
- Rituals may include business formalities, ceremonies (such as performance awards), 'pizza Fridays' and so on.
- Beliefs and values will be both expressed (in corporate mottos and marketing) and underlying (eg in attitude to risk or quality, employee relations, and the importance given to empowerment, teamwork and so on).

2.10 The corporate culture may embrace positive values such as quality and excellence, innovation and social responsibility – or may tolerate negative behaviours such as absenteeism, cutting corners and office politics. One of the key tasks of management is to shape (and if necessary, change) the culture in directions that will help the organisation to function and compete in its market. However, it is important to note that an organisation's culture is also partly shaped by its environment, as it will adopt elements of the other cultural spheres (nation, region and industry sector) in which it operates.

The impact of cultural factors on purchasing

2.11 Cultural factors may influence purchasing (and other organisational processes) in a number of ways.

2.12 Organisations will have to adapt their products and services to the culture of their market (or different market segments), and this will impact on the materials and other inputs required. These cultural factors may change over time. Think how the materials specifications of clothing manufacturers have changed, say, with value-driven changes in demand for animal fur or organically grown cotton. Or how food specifications have changed with growing awareness of obesity and food intolerance issues, or growing ethnic and religious groups with special dietary preferences.

2.13 Organisations may need to adapt their marketing and supply chain management to culture-driven changes, trends and fashions. You should be able to identify a range of such 'hot' cultural topics in your country or region. Here are some obvious examples.

- Growing public concern about environmental and ethical issues. So, for example, purchasers will need to select 'green' suppliers, utilise 'green' materials, implement recycling policies; monitor supplier performance in relation to ethical labour practices; or broaden the supply base in order to comply with diversity policies. The organisation as a whole may seek to develop eco-friendly and Fair Trade products to satisfy a growing market demand, and may seek to position itself as a socially responsible producer and employer.
- Growing concern for fitness and health. Food producers may have to modify their products (and purchasers their inputs), in order to make them low-fat-low-salt or otherwise healthier. There is an increasing market for sports-related and health-related goods and services. Employers may have to formulate work-life balance or corporate health programmes in order to retain quality employees.
- Growing use of personal electronic devices (such as mobile phones, MP3 players, digital cameras, palm-top computers – or all four rolled into one). This has opened new markets for some producers (eg Apple moving into mobile telecom with the iPhone) and all but destroyed the market for others (eg photographic processing and portable compact disc players). It has also altered the way organisations promote their products (eg with entertainment 'content' or SMS text messaging).

2.14 The organisation will reflect its national culture *and* will have its own organisation culture: even the purchasing function itself may have a distinctive culture (differing from the sales and marketing function, say). Some organisations may expect a flexible 'can do' attitude to price, customisation and delivery from purchasers and their suppliers, for example, while others may be more bureaucratic, bound by rules and procedures. Changes in purchasing policy and practice will be hard to sustain, if they do not 'fit' – and are therefore not supported or reinforced by – the corporate culture.

2.15 Purchasers may need to be particularly aware of cultural differences for cross-cultural or international teamworking and supplier management. 'Business gifts' which are considered essential in one culture, for example, may be interpreted as 'bribes' in another. (This will be discussed later in this chapter.) Similarly, marketers will need to be aware of the different values, tastes and preferences of overseas customers, and adapt products and messages accordingly.

3 Demographic and socio-economic factors

Demographics

3.1 Demography is the study of population and population trends. Demographic data is useful for purchasing (and business in general) because the population represents the source of demand for goods and services (and hence input requirements). The structure of the population has implications for demand in particular markets or market segments. Think of the effect that an increasingly *ageing* population would have on the business – and purchasing spend – of a childcare provider, or an aged care provider, a toy manufacturer, or the NHS. Think of the effect of an increasing *ethnically diverse* population on a food retailer or restaurateur; or the effect of increasing numbers of *single-person households* on the way goods are portioned and packaged...

3.2 The population also represents a source of skilled labour, which may affect purchasing recruitment – and also supply prices (as a cost of production for suppliers). Think of the effect on a rural employer in an area where employment-age people are increasingly moving to the city, say; or of the effect on purchasing recruitment and training of increasing numbers of women entering the workforce.

3.3 So what are the key demographic trends at the moment, from a purchasing point of view?

Population size

3.4 Population size is important for a number of reasons. If the population is too small, it may have insufficient labour and skills to exploit its resources and provide necessary services. If a population is too large, it may make excessive demands on the country's physical environment and resources, or may create a demand for public services that the public or private sector may not be able to supply. More importantly, perhaps, is the rate of change in the size of a population, with the potential to create either of the above problems.

3.5 Changes in the rate of population growth are caused by factors such as changes in the birth rate (or fertility rate), changes in the death rate (or mortality rate) and changes in the rate of emigration (people leaving the country) and/or immigration (people coming into the country).

3.6 The long-term growth in the world's total population has been due mainly to the reduction in the mortality rate: improved medicine and hygiene have reduced early loss of life through disease and childbirth. However, less developed countries also have a high birth rate, while developed countries have a declining birth date (in some countries, below the 'replenishment' rate of two children per couple). Developed countries are therefore facing a situation in which they need to import labour, in order to maintain productivity: a key driver for immigration.

3.7 In the UK, the overall population is increasing, mainly due to immigration. The number of people who are economically active has also been increasing, mainly through women entering the paid workforce. Both these factors tend to boost demand for goods and services.

Age structure

3.8 However, in the long term, the UK working-age population is expected to *shrink.* Birth-rates have been falling and life expectancy has been rising, creating an increasingly *aged* population and workforce. A larger proportion of the population will be retirees, and dependent on the (relatively smaller) younger working population for national income – and pensions.

3.9 An ageing population will change patterns of demand: shrinking the youth market and growing the 'grey' market. So, for example, durability may replace fashionability as the key attribute of product design and the purchasing of materials and components. Distribution systems may increasingly favour home delivery, at the expense of inner city or out-of-town retail outlets. Renewed emphasis may be placed on value-for-money products, with a pressure on purchasing to reduce costs.

3.10 An ageing population may also impact on labour supply: forcing firms to pay more for young workers, or to retrain and retain older workers – or to outsource activities to economies with younger and lower-cost labour pools (in which purchasing may play a part). Age discrimination in recruitment was outlawed in the UK for the first time in October 2006, partly in recognition of the need for greater acceptance of mature-age workers.

Regional distribution

3.11 There have been significant changes, over time, in where people choose to live and work. The UK has seen a shift from urban areas to non-metropolitan regions, but this trend may reverse as the government pushes local authorities to create or expand towns. In other countries, such as Australia, there is a problem with young people moving from the country into cities, eroding rural economies and threatening agricultural production. These sorts of trends affect public service provision and infrastructure, as well as patterns of regional demands for goods: some small geographically isolated communities may not be profitable for banks or retail chains, for example.

Gender

3.12 The UK working population has become increasingly diverse in terms of gender, as legislation and changing social values have supported women's right to work. This has highlighted employment issues such as equal opportunity and equal pay. It has also shifted gender roles in household buying, with women enjoying independent spending power. Nevertheless, markets may still usefully be segmented and targeted by sex, since women and men have distinct purchasing preferences and patterns.

Ethnicity

3.13 UK society as a whole has become increasingly diverse in terms of race and ethnic background. Few societies are now homogeneous in terms of culture or ethnic background, although there may be regional pockets where immigration and settlement have been more intense. Ethnic diversity has brought a wide variety of cultural factors and differences to bear on organisations.

- Creating markets for the foods and clothing styles of other cultures
- Creating cross-cultural and multi-cultural management situations within firms and supply chains
- Highlighting the need to reflect social diversity in the workforce and supply base.

Social units

3.14 More and more people in the UK live outside the traditional family unit. Over 30% of all households are now one-person households and around 10% are lone-parent families (mostly women). Grown-up children tend to stay at home longer, for economic reasons. Many families are 'blended' through divorce and remarriage. These kinds of changes will be reflected in the demand for products (eg single-serve packaged foods, and convenience items for 'time-poor' households) and in working arrangements (eg family friendly policies and part-time working to allow lone parents to participate in the workforce).

Socio-economic class

3.15 Definitions of *social class* are commonly derived from demographic factors including wealth or income, educational attainment and occupational status. Some classifications you may have heard

10

of include: lower/working-class (producers of goods and services), middle class (managers and organisers) and upper class (titled landowners and the very wealthy); or A, B, C1 (upper, middle and lower middle class), C2 and D (skilled and unskilled working class) and E (casual workers and welfare dependents).

3.16 The class structure of society will determine the level of demand for goods and services (and hence inputs), because of different classes' spending power, and what they spend their money on.

4 Corporate social responsibility and ethics

Business ethics

4.1 'Ethics' are simply a set of moral principles or values about what constitutes 'right' and 'wrong' behaviour. For individuals and groups, these often reflect the assumptions and beliefs of the families, national cultures and educational environments in which their ideas developed. Ethics are also shaped more deliberately by public and professional bodies, in the form of agreed principles and guidelines which are designed to protect society's best interests.

4.2 An exam question may pose a scenario in which ethical issues arise. The ethical environment includes factors such as: the core ethical values of the organisation and wider society; particular issues which raise ethical concern (eg supplier or worker exploitation, animal testing or the potential for fraud in purchasing); relevant ethical frameworks (eg Fair Trading certification, a corporate Code of Conduct or the CIPS Code of Ethics); and other pressures towards ethical behaviour (eg pressure groups, consumer support for ethical brands, or consumer boycott of allegedly unethical brands).

4.3 Ethical issues may affect purchasing at three levels. At the *macro* level, there are the issues of the role of business and capitalism in society: the debate about globalisation, the exploitation of workers, the impacts of industrialisation on the environment and so on. This is the sphere addressed by the Ethical Trading Initiative, for example: an alliance of companies, non-governmental organisations and trade unions committed to working together to promote internationally-agreed principles of ethical trade and employment.

4.4 At the *corporate* level, there are the issues which face individual organisations as they interact with their stakeholders. Some of these matters will be covered by legislative and regulatory requirements, and an organisation may have a 'compliance based' approach to ethics which strives merely to uphold these minimal requirements. The sphere generally referred to as **corporate social responsibility** covers policies which the organisation adopts for the good and wellbeing of stakeholders, taking a more proactive 'integrity based' approach: voluntarily seeking to 'do the right thing' in a given situation. This includes issues such as environmental protection and sustainability, fair trading, impact minimisation and community investment.

4.5 At the *individual* level, there are the issues which face purchasers within the organisation and supply chain: refusing to be party to fraud, say; not discriminating in the award of tenders; or deciding whether to accept gifts or hospitality from suppliers which might be perceived as an attempt to influence the placing of a contract. This is the sphere which is often covered in Codes of Ethics, such as that published by CIPS for its members. You should read through the CIPS code, if you haven't already done so.

Corporate social responsibility (CSR)

4.6 The term 'corporate social responsibility' is used to describe a wide range of obligations that an organisation may feel it has towards its secondary stakeholders, or the society in which it operates. It is sometimes expressed in terms of minimising **externalities**: the costs of business activities which are not reflected in the costing of a product or service and paid for by consumers, but which are borne by the wider community – such as the costs of pollution (and associated ill health), traffic congestion or environmental degradation.

4.7 One CIPS examiner has written that: 'CSR means the commitment to systematic consideration of the environmental, social and cultural aspects of an organisation's operations. This includes the key issues of sustainability, human rights, labour and community relations, and supplier and customer relations beyond legal obligations. The objective [is] to create long-term business value *and* contribute to improving the social conditions of the people affected by our operations.'

4.8 Any or all of the following considerations may be relevant in assessing a purchasing organisation's CSR obligations.

- *Sustainability* issues: conserving the world's limited natural resources (eg by minimising the use of non-renewable resources, minimising fuel use in transporting goods, or using recycled materials); and supporting small and local suppliers
- *Environmental* issues: 'green' materials, pollution control, waste management, the avoidance of environmental disfigurement, promoting recycling and so on – and ensuring that suppliers do the same
- *Ethical trading and business relationships*: ensuring product safety and quality for consumers; improving working and social conditions for employees and suppliers, particularly in developing nations; avoiding the abuse of buyer power to squeeze supplier prices (fair trading); upholding ethical employment practices (such as equal opportunities and employment protection); adherence to ethical codes and so on.

4.9 There are many ways in which a purchasing function can contribute to CSR objectives. For example, it can draw up and enforce codes of ethical practice in sourcing or adhere to the rules laid down in the CIPS ethical code, Ethical Trading Initiative or Fair Trade framework. It can encourage (or even insist on) ethical employment and/or environmental practices in its suppliers. It can adhere to health and safety, equal opportunities and other ethical practices in its own workplace and so on. (We will consider 'green' purchasing separately in Chapter 9.)

Why should an organisation set ethical standards and CSR objectives?

4.10 Milton Friedman took the view that 'the social responsibility of business is profit maximisation': providing a return on shareholders' investment. Spending funds on objectives *not* related to shareholder expectations is irresponsible, and the public interest is arguably already served by profit maximisation, through corporate taxes.

4.11 'Consequently,' argued Friedman, 'the only justification for social responsibility is *enlightened self interest*' (or ethical egoism) on the part of a business organisation. So how does CSR serve the interest of the firm?

- Law, regulation and Codes of Practice impose certain social responsibilities on organisations, and there are financial and operational penalties for failure to comply (eg 'polluter pays' taxes).

10

- Voluntary measures may enhance corporate image and build a positive brand. A commonly quoted example is the environmental and sustainability strategy adopted by The Body Shop. You might like to check out the website of the Medinge Group, which publishes profiles of each year's top *Brands with a Conscience*.
- Above-statutory provisions for employees and suppliers may be necessary to attract, retain and motivate them to provide quality service and commitment – particularly in competition with other employers or purchasers.
- Increasing consumer awareness of social responsibility issues creates a market demand for CSR (and the threat of boycott for irresponsible firms).
- Social responsibility helps to create a climate in which business can prosper in the long term. In the same way, ethical sourcing helps to create a climate in which mutually-beneficial long-term relationships with suppliers can be preserved.

5   Socio-cultural factors in international supply chains

Cultural differences

5.1   We noted earlier that *differences* in socio-cultural factors have a particular impact on purchasing in international or cross-cultural markets. In this section, we will briefly explore the sources of those differences, and what purchasing can do to overcome potential risks and problems arising from them.

5.2   Different countries (or world regions) have different cultural norms, values and assumptions which influence how they do business and manage people.

5.3   Culture researcher Geert Hofstede *(Cultures and Organisations)* formulated one of the most influential models of work-related cultural differences, identifying five key dimensions of difference between national cultures.

- *Power-distance:* the extent to which unequal distribution of power and status is accepted or involvement and participation expected
- *Uncertainty-avoidance:* the extent to which security, order, control and predictability are preferred to ambiguity, uncertainty, risk and change
- *Individualism:* the extent to which people prefer to live and work in individualist ('I') or collectivist ('we') ways
- *Masculinity:* the extent to which gender roles are distinct, and whether masculine values (assertiveness, competition) or feminine values (consensus, relationship) prevail.
- *Long-term orientation:* the extent to which thrift and perseverance are valued (long-term orientation) over respect for tradition, fulfilling solid obligations and protecting one's 'face' (short-term orientation).

5.4   You should be able to recognise the challenges faced by a purchaser in a country at one end of the spectrum, in dealing with a supplier at the other end of the spectrum, on each dimension. For example, a purchaser in a low uncertainty-avoidance culture such as the UK will be flexible about procedure and forthright about disagreements: a supplier from a high uncertainty-avoidance culture such as Japan may be uncomfortable working without written rules and procedures, and may be offended or stressed by disagreement.

5.5   You may also be able to think of more specific examples of cultural differences, to do with aspects such as the following.

- Attitudes to the participation of women in business. (Equal opportunity is less of a value in some Middle Eastern and Latin cultures, for example.)
- Negotiating and conflict styles. Many Asian cultures, for example, have a strong reluctance to lose 'face' or respect, or to cause others to do so, and are therefore reluctant to criticise or challenge in public
- Decision-making styles. Many Asian cultures seek consensus or group agreement in decision-making, rather than leader-imposed or majority-rule decisions.
- The perceived propriety of business gifts and hospitality. These may be considered an important sign of mutual respect in some cultures – where in the West they are regarded as unprofessional and unethical attempts to influence decisions, and are often covered in corporate Ethical Codes. This may be a particular issue for purchasers.
- Business customs and formalities. Each culture has its business rituals: eg the importance of business cards in Japan, the importance of social conversation prior to getting down to business in Middle Eastern cultures, or the comparative informality of interpersonal dealings in North America.

Other differences impacting on international sourcing

5.6 There may be a number of other potential differences to take into account.

- Differences in working practices, which can be a source of misunderstanding or frustration for overseas purchasers and managers. Examples might include long lunch breaks in some European countries, and greater (or less) emphasis on worker involvement in decision-making.
- Different standard working hours, wage rates and conditions of employment. This can pose ethical issues and reputational risks for purchasers. Oxfam faced severe embarrassment, for example, when it was found that its overseas suppliers of 'Make Poverty History' armbands were exploiting their workers, by Western standards.
- Different legal and regulatory regimes (eg on quality standards, worker terms and conditions, health and safety, intellectual property protection and so on). The rules in a different country may be more stringent than at home (creating compliance difficulties) – but are often *less* stringent (creating quality, ethical and reputational risks for the purchaser). US toy makers, for example, have recently fallen foul of the less stringent regulation of their Chinese subcontractors: many toys had to be recalled owing to the use of toxic lead paint (banned in the US and EU).
- Language differences, which may create a barrier to effective communication in materials specification, negotiation and contracting, relationship management and so on
- Differences in communication infrastructure and tools (eg lack of internet, fax or even phone access for doing business) – an effect made more acute by possible differences in time zone (requiring communication tools for 24/7 dealings, such as email)
- Different education and skill levels and emphases, and different professional qualification standards: this may affect the selection and management of outsource providers, for example
- Different standard business terms (eg credit periods, standard contract clauses, payment methods) and so on.

Managing diversity and socio-cultural differences

5.7 Schneider & Barsoux *(Managing Across Cultures)* argue that 'rather than knowing what to do in Country X, or whether national or functional cultures are more important in multi-cultural teams, what is necessary is to know *how to assess the potential impact* of culture, national or otherwise, on performance.'

5.8 At the organisational and departmental level, there should be a plan to evaluate this potential impact and to implement programmes to encourage: awareness of areas of difference and sensitivity; behavioural flexibility (being able to adapt in different situations and relationships); and constructive communication, conflict resolution and problem-solving, where differences emerge.

Chapter summary

- Factors in the socio-cultural environment include: demographics, socio-economics, social infrastructure, culture, ethics, consumer trends and human resource management. All these factors can influence the demand for goods and trading and employment relationships. Particular challenges are posed by changes and differences.
- Culture comprises the shared ways of behaving and understanding that are distinctive to a particular group of people. Trompenaars suggests that culture operates on three levels: outward expressions, values and beliefs, underlying assumptions. Only the first of these is outwardly observable.
- Organisational culture is 'a pattern of beliefs and expectations shared by an organisation's members, which produce norms that powerfully shape the behaviour of individuals and groups in the organisation'. More simply, it is 'the way we do things around here'.
- A number of demographic factors influence purchasers: population size; age structure; regional distribution of the population; gender; ethnicity; social units; and socio-economic class.
- Ethics are moral principles or values about right and wrong. They apply to purchasing at a macro, corporate and individual level. Corporate social responsibility (CSR) describes the range of obligations that an organisation might have towards its secondary stakeholders.
- International trade poses challenges from differences in culture, language, local working practices and business customs, different legal regimes and communications.

Self-test questions

Numbers in brackets refer to paragraphs where you can check your answers

1 Define 'culture' and identify its different manifestations, according to Trompenaars. (2.1, 2.2)

2 What is organisation culture? (2.8)

3 List three current demographic trends and explain their impact on purchasing. (Section 3)

4 How do definitions of socio-economic class impact on purchasing? (3.16)

5 Give two examples of (a) macro and (b) individual ethical issues. (4.3, 4.5)

6 What are 'externalities'? (4.6)

7 Cite three arguments in support of CSR. (4.11)

8 Explain the Hofstede model of cultural differences. (5.3)

9 List four socio-cultural differences which pose a challenge for international purchasing. (5.4, 5.5)

10 How might 'communication' be a point of difference with an impact on international purchasing? (5.6)

10

CHAPTER 11

Technological Factors

Assessment criteria and indicative content

Although technological factors are one of the STEEPLE factors referred to in unit content 3.1, there is no separate caption relating to this area (as there is for all the other elements of STEEPLE). In case this is simply an oversight, we have provided coverage in this final chapter.

Section headings

1. The technological environment
2. Technological development
3. Developments in ICT
4. E-sourcing and e-procurement

Introduction

In this chapter, we look at technological factors, which have to do not just with machines, but with the choices organisations have to make around automation, computerisation, innovation, knowledge and change in business processes.

We start, as in previous chapters, by giving an overview of the impact of different technology applications on products, markets and business processes.

We then go on to discuss how new technologies develop, how nations differ in the extent of their technological development or sophistication, how development can be encouraged – and how new technology may be seen as a drawback as well as a benefit.

In the final sections, we explore some of the key developments in technologies relevant to purchasing, and how they are being applied, finishing with a brief survey of purchasing technology: e-sourcing and e-procurement systems.

1   The technological environment

What is technology?

1.1   Technology refers not just to 'machinery', but to means and methods of production, including: the apparatus (tools and equipment), techniques (ways of using tools, work methods) and organisation (how tasks are structured and resources deployed). When we talk about the technological environment, therefore, we are usually referring to:

- Developments in mechanised, automated or computerised ways of doing things (apparatus and techniques): for example, email, the internet, computer-aided design and manufacture (CAD/CAM) or radio frequency identification (RFID); *and*
- The changes to business structures and processes that those developments make possible

(organisation): for example, electronic communication, e-procurement, integrated materials planning, just in time supply, stock and delivery tracking, virtual teamworking and so on.

An overview of technology's impact on purchasing

1.2 Technological developments have a range of impacts on business and purchasing activity.

1.3 Automation and computerisation raise productivity by allowing faster, more accurate, more consistent work than human beings can achieve alone. A supplier with access to advanced design, manufacturing, goods handling and transport technology should be able to fulfil orders faster, more cheaply and with more consistent (though not necessarily higher) quality.

1.4 Technology opens up new *product* markets through the potential for product innovation: think of the relatively new markets for digital cameras, MP3 players, music and book downloads, plasma TVs and so on. These new markets impact on purchasing by creating new sourcing requirements.

1.5 Technology also opens up new *supply* markets, eg by giving purchasers access to information on international suppliers via the internet, and facilitating communication and transaction processing. Technology may also be a differentiating or cost-saving factor, lowering barriers to entry and allowing small new producers or service providers access to established markets.

1.6 Technology changes business processes. It may be used to perform operational functions more safely (eg automated production and materials handling) or easily (eg recording and tracking stock movements using barcoding or RFID). In recent decades, it has changed both production processes and supply and distribution processes.

- Production processes, with an emphasis on labour-saving equipment and machinery – impacting purchasing through the need for investment appraisal and capital purchases. Examples include the increasing use of automated (or robotic) production, computer-aided design and manufacture, computerised quality and process monitoring and so on.
- Supply and distribution processes. Examples include: access to new global supply and product markets through e-commerce and faster transport; electronic sourcing and procurement systems (for e-auctions, order cycle processing, delivery tracking and so on); and new methods of service delivery (such as ATM machines, online entertainment ticketing and online banking).

1.7 Technology changes the amount of labour and types of skills required by businesses (eg through the use of labour-saving automation) and how they can be organised and managed (eg the use of information and communication technology to facilitate off-site and mobile working, and 'virtual' teamworking). This may in turn support the use of outsourcing and subcontracting, which may be driven and managed by the purchasing function. It may also create a changing skill profile for purchasers (eg use of e-procurement tools).

1.8 Technology influences the competition in an industry. It impacts on competitive forces: for example, by raising entry barriers (eg if high investment in technology is required to enter the market); lowering entry barriers (eg by giving new players a differentiating advantage); or altering the balance of power between buyers and suppliers (eg by making it easier for buyers to switch, because they have more information – or harder, because they are 'locked in' to a shared computer network, say).

The impact of information and communication technology (ICT)

1.9 Information and communication technology (computers + telecommunications) has had a particular impact on purchasing.

- Dramatically increasing the speed of communication and information processing. Real-time answers to enquiries, updating of information and processing of transactions can be conducted via a computer network or the internet.

- Offering wider access to environmental and supply market information (especially from global sources). The internet offers constant access to formal information resources (in the form of websites, databases, libraries, expert agencies and so on) and informal resources in the form of network contacts. This has had the effect of opening up new supply markets, by giving purchasers access to information about suppliers and supply markets worldwide.

- Facilitating 24-hour, 7-day, global business. The internet and email allow companies to offer service and maintain communication across office hours, international time zones and geographical distances.

- Supporting paperless communications (eg electronic mail messages), business transactions (eg online ordering and payment) and service delivery (eg online ticket reservations, information and education services, and so on). Information storage and retrieval is less wasteful of physical space and resources – and of administrative time.

- Offering opportunities for cost savings, through a wider supply base, streamlined processes and lower prices (eg via e-auctions)

- Freeing up buyers' time – previously taken up by routine and repetitive clerical tasks – for creative, strategic and relational aspects of their roles

- Enhancing management information (eg via databases and systems which record, store and analyse a wide range of transaction, business and environmental data).

- Creating 'virtual' supplier relationships, teams and organisations, by making location irrelevant to the process of collaboration.

2 Technological development

New technology development

2.1 Technological development may mean new technological innovations or improvements in various directions, such as added speed or power, increased miniaturisation, increased performance, quality and reliability, lower prices and costs and so on. (Think about how personal computing and mobile phones have changed in the last few years, for example.) Obviously this is a vast topic, and we can only a highlight a few points of interest: your own experience, and attention to media stories, will suggest many more examples.

2.2 The Austrian economist **Joseph Schumpeter** distinguished three stages in the process by which new technologies develop and become adopted by an industry or market.

- *Invention:* scientifically or technically new ideas are devised for a product or process.
- *Innovation:* the ideas are developed into marketable products and processes, which are introduced to the market. Innovation or product development includes prototyping, feasibility studies, technical and market testing and so on.
- *Diffusion* (or dissemination): the innovation proves successful and gradually comes to be widely available for use, through increasing adoption by individuals and organisations – which makes them increasingly cost-effective over time.

11

All three stages are required for what we call 'technological change', resulting in the cumulative economic and environmental impacts of new technology.

2.3   Schumpeter's distinctions helpfully highlight the fact that innovation is more than just 'new ideas': application and market success are necessary to create genuine technology development. In other words, the real impact of new technology on an economy occurs at the diffusion stage, where technologies are introduced and used.

2.4   It is worth noting, however, that this model suggests a linear process from invention to diffusion. In fact, it is a cyclical process: once an innovation is introduced into a market and deployed in practice, there will be a flow of feedback information which will usually stimulate further technical development and adaptation. This suggests that, in order to stimulate technological development, investment is required not just in invention, research and development – but in getting technology to market.

2.5   Schumpeter went on to analyse the effect of technological change on the performance of an economy. In the 1920s, Nikolai Kondratieff had identified peaks and troughs in economic prosperity in major Western economies (which you might equate to the business cycles discussed in Chapter 6). Schumpeter observed that the upswings (or 'upwaves') in economic activity coincide with major technological innovations, and the 'downwaves' coincide with lack of further innovation (once previous innovations have become an accepted part of the economy and no longer yield dynamic improvements). There was a major upswing towards the end of the 20th century, for example, resulting from developments in information and communication technology.

Technological development and product lifecycles

2.6   As we saw in an earlier chapter, the product lifecycle (PLC) is a model which compares the 'shelf life' of a product to the life of a living organism, which goes through various stages. The basic principle of the PLC is that products have a finite life.

2.7   Once a product reaches the stage of maturity, and is faced with the prospect of decline, organisations need to protect their profits and competitive position by either of the following measures.

- Introducing new products, so that as one product declines, another reaches peak profitability in its place *or*
- 'Refreshing' the mature product: re-inventing or modifying it, so that it can be re-introduced to the market as 'new and improved', renewing the lifecycle.

2.8   Schumpeter argued that innovative organisations refresh existing products before they reach decline, hastening the obsolescence of the old product – and therefore shortening the product lifecycle. (You might think of new versions of computer operating software, for example, or new 'generations' of iPods: no-one wants the old versions once the new ones come out, so the old version quickly declines.)

2.9   Dynamic and innovative technological environments support faster and more frequent product development and updating: new features, greater miniaturisation, better recyclability and so on. The availability of new and updated products sends existing products into decline more quickly, so product lifecycles in these environments are generally getting shorter. Bradley *(The Purchasing Environment)* claims that the product lifecycle of a car in Europe is 5–7 years (because new models and features are constantly coming onto the market), while in developing countries it is often more than 30 years (because the pace of innovation is slower).

2.10 Frequent product innovation and modification requires flexible purchasing strategies – among other challenges.

The pace of technological development in different economies

2.11 The pace of technological development varies from economy to economy, according to factors such as the following.

- The availability of infrastructure (eg telecommunications cabling or band width)
- The extent of government investment in innovation and infrastructure development
- Government support and incentives for private sector investment (eg innovation forums or tax incentives)
- Education and research support from the academic community – which also requires investment in universities and labs, eg in the form of research and innovation grants
- The availability of markets in which to deploy and test new technologies (which, as we have seen, is how innovation really impacts on an economy)
- The extent and pace of cultural adaptation (eg the willingness of a society to accept new technologies, and its ability to afford technology products). Some cultures may adopt new technology products early; some may prefer to wait and see, or wait until the prices come down; some may prize tradition so highly that new technologies are actively resisted.

2.12 Developing economies often lack the resources to invest in systematic technology innovation and adoption. This hampers their economic development still further, since technological advancement is one of the defining factors in economic development. Even within rapidly developing economies, such as China, there may be regional variations in infrastructure and access, due to geographic isolation or lack of resources.

Technology transfer

2.13 If an organisation or developed nation wishes to trade with a less advanced country, it may need to boost its technological capability. The process whereby more advanced nations share their technology with less developed economies is called **technology transfer**.

2.14 Technology transfer may take place in a variety of ways. Individual trading partners may supply their subsidiaries, suppliers or joint venture partners in developing nations with any of the following.

- Technological knowledge, management expertise, consultancy and training
- Investment or co-investment funding for new technology or research and development.
- Access to design patents for new technology products and processes (so that they do not have to be developed from scratch)
- Finished technology products, machinery and tools – such as computers, mobile phones, production equipment, vehicles and so on.

2.15 International agencies, or national governments, may similarly provide: consultancy; education and training; business networking opportunities (to encourage the sharing of technological know-how and innovation ideas); and/or investment or co-investment funding in the form of grants or loans (often for research and infrastructure projects).

11

Government support for technology development

2.16 National governments frequently aim both to invest in technology research and infrastructure, and to encourage the private sector to do so, in order to boost national competitiveness. In the UK, for example, HM Treasury offers tax incentives for investment in research and development activity, and for small business investment in ICT.

2.17 The UK government's pioneering Global Watch Service was designed to help UK businesses to identify and access innovative technologies and practices from overseas, but it was replaced in April 2007 by a simpler and more streamlined scheme called Knowledge Transfer Networks (KTNs). KTNs were set up by government, industry and academia to facilitate the transfer of knowledge between the industrial and scientific sectors.

2.18 The Department for Innovation, Universities and Skills (DIUS) is responsible for supporting science, research and innovation through education and skills training. It is also responsible for allocating the science budget into research.

2.19 In addition to direct investment in technology development, governments can create *demand* for technology products and innovation – for example, by public spending on defence or e-procurement – which will stimulate private sector research and development.

2.20 Private sector firms also stimulate invention and innovation in various ways: by providing experts to innovation think tanks, by inviting contributions from independent inventors, and by making innovative products and processes available in the market.

Caution about technological development

2.21 Organisations can get very enthusiastic about the possibilities of new technology. However, they must recognise that a given technology may not be the most effective, or cost-effective, solution to every business challenge. Here are some drawbacks of technology.

- High capital investment and set-up costs (design and development, hardware and software costs) – which may put more sophisticated applications (such as electronic data interchange or EDI) beyond the reach of small firms.
- High initial learning curve costs: training of users, cost of initial errors while users learn the system, potential confusion of running the system in parallel with old methods during the initial period
- Reliability issues, especially at an early stage of development, with the risk of 'bugs' in the software and initial teething troubles. Reliability may continue to be a problem, however, with the risks of network breakdown, power failure or viruses contaminating the system – and this can often cause chaos if the firm has become dependent on the technology (eg to communicate with suppliers or access information), with no backup systems in place.
- Compatibility issues, if the system is required to work together with the different systems of suppliers, say – or if key suppliers do not have access to the technology.

2.22 In addition, as we noted earlier, the pace of technological development varies from economy to economy: there may be large variations in infrastructure sophistication, compatibility and technology access and adoption in international markets.

2.23 There may also be ethical issues in the adoption of technology by a business.

- Smaller suppliers may not be able to afford to invest in collaborative technologies (such as an EDI network for transaction processing), and it may be unethical – and damaging to long-term relationships – to force them to do so.
- Automation of processes previously carried out by people has implications for staffing, and these will need to be handled responsibly: redundancies should be minimised (eg by retraining and redeploying staff, or freezing recruitment in advance to let normal resignations and retirements reduce staff numbers) and carefully managed to minimise hardship and conflict.
- Any significant change can be a source of insecurity, resistance and temporary loss of performance (as people learn new ways of doing things). Technological changes require stakeholder education, consultation and management.

3 Developments in ICT

3.1 Computerisation has been applied to a wide range of areas – some of which you will be using in everyday life. The following is just a brief survey of some of the tools which have emerged, with particular relevance to purchasing.

Operational systems

3.2 Operational systems are very diverse, including: materials and production planning systems, stock control systems, computer-aided design and manufacture (including robotics), and warehouse systems (including automated materials handling and stock/delivery tracking).

Point of sale and tracking systems

3.3 *Point of sale devices* involve the use of barcoding and radio frequency identification (RFID) tagging to record sales at point-of-sale terminals, which are linked to IT systems. Electronic point of sale (EPOS) systems can be used to track product sales, stock availability and location. They can also be connected to inventory management systems (for automatic stock replenishment), payment systems (via electronic funds transfer) and management information systems (for sales analysis, demand forecasting and inventory).

3.4 *RFID* is perhaps the 'hottest' technology in this area. EPOS and inventory control systems have for some years used barcoding as the main technology for automatic data capture. However, the use of RFID tags (transponders) offers significant advantages, compared to conventional optical scanning of barcodes.

- The tag doesn't have to be scanned or 'seen' by the reader: it can be used for updating inventory of moving and 'hidden' items in complex storage and transport environments.
- Data can be flexibly interrogated and updated for stock control, re-order triggering and so on.
- A *CIPS Practice Guide* argues that RFID can offer improved product availability; improved utilisation of resources; lower total operating costs; and enhanced safety, security and quality control.

Communications and relationship management systems

3.5 You should be able to draw on your own personal experience of 'newish' (and constantly developing) communications tools and systems, including: email; electronic banking and funds transfers (used in business for direct payments to supplier or employee bank accounts); mobile telecommunications and mobile computing (eg using mobile phones and palmtop computers to connect to the internet).

3.6 More specialised business-use communications systems include **electronic data interchange** or EDI (direct computer-to-computer communication within a network). This has been one of the most important developments in IT for purchasing. Instead of exchanging paper-based documents, inter-organisational enquiries and transactions are sent via cable or telecommunications links, directly from one computer system to another. EDI can be used for the following purposes.

- Query handling: sending marketing, transaction and technical information (product and price details, technical product or process specifications, terms and conditions of trade)
- Transaction handling: generating quotes, purchase orders, delivery instructions, receipt acknowledgements, invoices and so on
- Funds transfer (electronic payments to supplier or employee accounts, using direct transfer or credit card).

3.7 Communications developments (particularly the internet, email, web-casting and video-conferencing) have also facilitated 'virtual' teamworking and organisation. **Virtual teams** are interconnected groups of people who may not be present in the same office and may even be in different areas of the world, but who use ICT links to: share information and tasks (eg technical support provided by a supplier); make joint decisions (eg on quality assurance or staff training); and fulfil the collaborative functions of a team.

3.8 Partners in the supply chain, for example, can use ICT links to access and share up-to-date product, customer, stock and delivery information (eg using web-based databases and tracking systems). Electronic meeting management systems allow virtual meeting participants to talk and listen to each other on teleconference lines, while sharing data and using electronic 'whiteboards' on their PCs or laptops. This supports enhanced supplier relationships and the management of outsourcing, particularly international outsourcing (or 'offshoring'): you don't need to be within reach of people to monitor their performance, stay in touch – or even have meetings.

Management information

3.9 Management information is data collected, processed and formatted in such a way as to be useful to managers to aid them in planning, control and decision-making. Management information tools include the following.

- Databases and database management: capturing and storing data (eg on customers, products and inventory, suppliers or transactions in progress) in a structured way, so that they can be shared by different users, and interrogated flexibly for a variety of applications.
- Decision support systems: eg spreadsheets and computer models, used to examine the effect of different inputs and scenarios on the outcomes of a plan or decision.
- Management information systems: integrated systems for recording, storing and analysing a wide range of sales, purchase, point-of-sale, inventory, maintenance, HR, financial and business intelligence data, to support management decision-making.

3.10 Database systems now have widespread application in business. Databases can be interrogated and the data analysed (using a process called 'datamining') for applications such as: identifying the best suppliers (for purchase decisions) or customers (for targeted marketing effort); developing the supplier or customer base (by identifying potentially valuable contacts and relationships to pursue); and enhancing supplier and customer relationships, by using information to personalise, target and streamline communications.

3.11 Perhaps most importantly, databases ensure continuity of knowledge, service and relationships. People move on, and have limited memory capacity at best: databases allow historical and current data about supplier performance, customer preferences and inventory levels to be stored and retrieved as needed.

The internet and e-commerce

3.12 The internet is a worldwide computer network allowing computers to communicate via telecommunications links. The network can also be accessed from laptop computers, personal digital assistants (such as Palm Pilots) and 3G mobile phones. The internet has exploded in the last decade as a business tool, for:

- Marketing: supporting advertising, direct marketing, customer communication, public relations and market research (eg using online surveys and browsing or transaction histories).
- Direct distribution: of products (through online product ordering, or the downloading of electronic products such as music, video or educational content) and services (eg information, ticketing, consultancy and e-learning).
- Customer service and technical support: through email enquiries, FAQs (frequently asked questions), access to database information etc.
- Partnership development: through better information-sharing and communication with suppliers and business networks.

3.13 The term 'e-commerce' (short for electronic commerce) refers to business transactions carried out online via ICT – usually the internet. E-commerce has facilitated direct marketing, linking customers direct with suppliers. It is a means of automating business transactions and workflows, and usually a means of streamlining and improving them. (However, it must be remembered that at some point, goods may have to be physically transported from the producer to the purchaser – and at this point, the speed of transaction-processing may not be matched by the speed of delivery.)

3.14 For the purchasing function, the internet has provided particular benefits.

- Wider choice of suppliers, including global and small suppliers. (Purchasing professionals still have to make strategic and tactical choices: ICT merely provides better-quality information for doing this.)
- Savings in procurement costs, through electronic communication, greater accuracy and electronic transaction processing. In a research project in 1997, management consultants McKinsey noted that the biggest effect of the internet for business overall is the huge saving in transaction and interaction costs – the costs of 'the searching, coordinating and monitoring that people and companies do when they exchange goods, services or ideas'.
- Support for low inventory and efficient stock turnover (eg just in time supply).
- Improved supply chain relationships and coordination, arising from better data-sharing.

Intranets and extranets

3.15 An *intranet* is a set of networked and/or internet-linked computers, which is accessible only to authorised users within the same organisation or work group.

11

3.16 Intranets are used in employee communication: only employees are able to access relevant web pages and internal email facilities. Intranets may provide employees with access to a wide range of internal information: performance databases and reporting systems; employment and training information; noticeboards; internal email facilities; mailings of employee newsletters and work updates; internal training software and so on.

3.17 An *extranet* is an intranet that has been extended to give selected outside users authorised access to particular areas or levels of the organisation's website or information network. Examples include the registered-user-only pages of corporate websites and the member-only pages of professional bodies' websites (such as CIPS).

3.18 Extranets are particularly useful tools for customer and supplier relationship management. They may be used to publish news updates and technical briefings which may be of use to clients or supply chain partners; to exchange transaction data and messages; or to share training resources (as part of collaborative quality management, say).

4 E-sourcing and e-procurement

E-sourcing

4.1 CIPS defines e-sourcing as 'using the internet to make decisions and form strategies regarding how and where services or products are obtained'. In other words, it concerns the first part of the purchasing cycle from need recognition to contract: purchasing research, definition of requirements, tendering, supplier selection and contract award. This technology is mainly used by specialist buyers.

4.2 E-sourcing may take a number of forms, depending on the purchasing methods used.

- *Electronic catalogues*. Suppliers exhibit their products in electronic catalogues, and buyers work with those details (product specifications, prices etc) to purchase materials and services.
- *E-tendering*, using electronic RFQ (request for quotation) procedures. RFQs and specifications are posted online or sent to different suppliers, and competing bids for the contract are received and evaluated electronically.
- *E-auctions*, where a seller offers goods for sale and potential buyers bid competitively: all bids are 'open', so buyers may raise their offers during the auction; the highest bid at the time limit wins. (You may be familiar with this system from e-Bay, for example.)
- *Reverse auctions*, where a *buyer* specifies its needs/demands, and suppliers submit quotes competitively: again, all bids are open, so suppliers may lower their prices during the auction, and the lowest bid at the time limit wins.
- *Market exchanges*: electronic marketplaces where multiple buyers and sellers meet and exchange goods.

Advantages of e-sourcing

4.3 Various benefits have been claimed for the use of e-sourcing, especially in the public sector: Table 11.1.

Table 11.1 *Advantages of e-sourcing (in the public sector)*

BENEFIT	EXPLANATION
Process efficiencies	Reducing time and effort spent on tendering and contract management; reduced paperwork; fewer human errors
Compliance	Eg with the provisions of the Efficiency Review and the National Procurement Strategy for Local Government
Cost savings	Reducing the direct costs of tendering (for both buyer and suppliers); more efficient comparison, supporting savings through competition
Collaboration	Making it easier for purchasers to work together on common sourcing projects across different departments and regions: creating 'virtual buying organisations' to increase bargaining power
Strategic focus	Allowing purchasing professionals to focus on value-added and strategic procurement activity (such as supplier screening, supply base development and relationship management), rather than administration

E-procurement

4.4 CIPS defines e-procurement as 'using the internet to operate the transactional aspects of requisitioning, authorising, ordering, receipting and payment processes for the required services or products'. In other words, it involves the 'purchase to pay' part of the purchasing cycle: from purchase approval to the receipt of the product, followed by payment. This technology makes it possible for users who are *not* purchasing specialists to manage the buying process according to systematic purchasing disciplines – so it is often used to devolve buying to user departments.

4.5 E-procurement tools include the following.

- *Desk-top procurement systems:* allowing users to place electronic orders with approved suppliers, within the framework of a supply contract already set up by the purchasing function
- *Electronic data interchange:* the exchange of transaction documents in a standardised electronic form, directly from a computer application in one organisation to an application in another
- *Online track and trace:* the ability to trace the location and progress of deliveries, using barcodes or RFID tagging and/or global positioning systems (GPS)
- *Electronic payment:* automated generation of invoices for orders (self-billing); matching of invoices with orders and goods received; payment by electronic funds transfer; or the use of credit-card style purchasing cards
- *Electronic point of sale (EPOS) systems:* getting sales and inventory updates from point of sale terminals, which may also trigger automatic re-ordering if stocks are low
- *Contract management systems:* electronic contracts; reporting of any performance discrepancies; contract updating and so on
- *Database information:* centrally stored and managed data concerning supply markets, customers, supplier performance or other areas, which can be updated and interrogated in real time.

4.6 The consequences of computerising purchasing systems can be dramatic. A UK government booklet *Supplying the Challenge*, for example, described the process at confectionery company Mars. 'Buyers have replaced paper and files with electronic information and links to company operational data: now the company is reaping the rewards through more co-ordinated –

11

increasingly pan-European – buying, better scheduled deliveries, and more information available more quickly to [internal] customers throughout the organisation. Everyone creating a requisition does so on a computer screen. Buying authorisations are registered on-screen and buyers create priced orders from the information brought together by the system. This alone saves huge amounts of time and money. Perhaps more important, the system helps Mars plan further ahead and control its purchasing better.'

4.7   An article in *Supply Management* cited the example of supermarket giant Sainsbury's which in the last decade has completely re-engineered its supply chain. Among other changes (involving the structure of the distribution system), Sainsbury's has fully automated two of its warehouses, in order to minimise human error and implement zero defect order fulfilment. It has also introduced real-time information and collaborative commerce across the extended supply chain. This includes:

- Computerised inventory management, to enhance control over the supplier-to-store replenishment network
- Data-mining applications, gathering information at point of sale, measuring on-shelf availability on an hour-by-hour basis, and facilitating real-time re-ordering.

4.8   You should gather your own examples of e-purchasing systems in action, from your own experience and from your reading in *Supply Management*.

Chapter summary

- Technology embraces apparatus, techniques and organisation. Technological change has had major impacts on purchasing and operations – and you should review these in detail.
- New technology develops in three stages: invention, innovation and diffusion. This happens at different rates in different economies, depending on infrastructure, support, investment and adoption. Developed nations can support developing nations via technology transfer.
- Despite the immense advantages of new technology, there are also (potentially) operational, financial and ethical drawbacks that must be considered.
- A number of key technological developments in relation to purchasing were discussed in Section 3 of this chapter: point of sale and tracking systems; communications and relationship management systems; management information systems; the internet, intranets and extranets.
- E-sourcing is the application of the internet to the pre-contract stages of the purchasing cycle, while e-procurement covers the purchase-to-pay stages of the cycle. Both offer benefits of a wider supply base, cost savings (through efficiency) and lower prices (eg through e-auctions).

 ## Self-test questions

Numbers in brackets refer to paragraphs where you can check your answers

1   Explain the impact of technology developments in opening up new markets. (1.4, 1.5)

2   Explain the impact of technology developments on business processes. (1.6)

3   Explain the impact of technology developments on competition. (1.8)

4   Explain the three stages of new technology development and innovation. (2.2)

5   Explain the impact of technology developments on product lifecycles. (2.9)

6   Identify three mechanisms of technology transfer. (2.14)

7   What are the potential drawbacks of technological change? (2.21)

8   What are (a) RFID and (b) intranets? (3.4, 3.15)

9   Give three examples of computerised applications supporting purchasing and operations management. (Section 3)

10   Give three examples of (a) e-sourcing and (b) e-procurement tools. (4.2, 4.5)

11

Subject Index